CONVEYANCING 2000

CONVEYANCING 2000

KENNETH G. C. REID WS

Professor of Property Law in the University of Edinburgh

and

GEORGE L. GRETTON WS

Lord President Reid Professor of Law in the University of Edinburgh

BUTTERWORTHS
2001

United Kingdom	Butterworths, a Division of Reed Elsevier (UK) Ltd, 4 Hill Street, EDINBURGH EH2 3JZ and Halsbury House, 35 Chancery Lane, LONDON WC2A 1EL
Australia	Butterworths, a Division of Reed International Books Australia Pty Ltd, CHATSWOOD, New South Wales
Canada	Butterworths Canada Ltd, MARKHAM, Ontario
Hong Kong	Butterworths Hong Kong, a Division of Reed Elsevier (Greater China) Ltd, HONG KONG
India	Butterworths India, NEW DELHI
Ireland	Butterworths (Ireland) Ltd, DUBLIN
Malaysia	Malayan Law Journal Sdn Bhd, KUALA LUMPUR
New Zealand	Butterworths of New Zealand Ltd, WELLINGTON
Singapore	Butterworths Asia, SINGAPORE
South Africa	Butterworths Publishers (Pty) Ltd, DURBAN
USA	Lexis Law Publishing, CHARLOTTESVILLE, Virginia

A CIP Catalogue record for this book is available from the British Library.

ISBN 0 406 94302 8

Typeset by Waverley Typesetters, Galashiels
Printed by Bell & Bain Ltd, Glasgow

Visit us at our website: http://www.butterworthsscotland.com

CONTENTS

PREFACE

Conveyancing 1999 was a survey of the developments in conveyancing law and practice during calendar year 1999. The present volume continues the story for the calendar year 2000, although it has also been possible to notice some developments from the first weeks of 2001.

The volume is divided into five parts. There is, first, a summary of all cases reported in 2000 (as well as a few decided in that year but not yet reported). The next two parts summarise, respectively, statutory developments during 2000 and other material of interest to conveyancers. Part IV, the longest, comprises a detailed commentary on selected issues arising from the first three parts. This includes an analysis of the Abolition of Feudal Tenure etc (Scotland) Act 2000. Finally, in Part V, there are two tables. The cumulative table of appeals is designed to facilitate moving from one annual volume to the next. For convenience of reference there is also a table of cases digested in *Conveyancing 1999* but reported, either for the first time or in an additional series, in 2000.

We do not seek to cover agricultural holdings, crofting, public sector tenancies (except the right-to-buy legislation), compulsory purchase or planning law. Otherwise our coverage is intended to be complete.

We are grateful to our colleague Alan Barr for contributing the section on the Finance Act 2000 which appears in Part II, and for help in other ways.

Kenneth G C Reid
George L Gretton
12 February 2001

TABLE OF CASES

TABLE OF STATUTES

TABLE OF STATUTORY INSTRUMENTS

PART I

CASES

There follows a digest of all significant cases in the general field of Conveyancing which were reported during 2000 in *Session Cases, Scots Law Times, Scottish Civil Law Reports, Greens Housing Law Reports,* and *Greens Weekly Digest.* It has also been possible to include a number of unreported cases. The final part of *Scottish Civil Law Reports* for 2000 was not published until 2001 and will be included in our 2001 Volume.

At the end of 2000 a most important collection, *Unreported Property Cases from the Sheriff Courts,* was published under the editorship of Professor Roderick Paisley and Sheriff Douglas Cusine. Naturally, the cases included in that volume go back a number of years. To have included all of them in the present work seemed both unnecessary and impracticable: unnecessary because Professor Paisley has provided his own most valuable commentary for each case, and impracticable because it would greatly increase the size of the present volume. Hence we have, albeit reluctantly, included only those cases in that collection which were decided in 2000.

MISSIVES

(1) Donald v Hutchinson 2000 SLT 963 (OH)

Condition 7 of an offer to buy a flat, subsequently part of the concluded bargain, provided that:

> There are no matters affecting the subjects or the larger premises of which the subjects form part which would require any form of repair, maintenance or attention known to the seller whether formally intimated or not affecting the subjects of sale or the premises of which the subjects of sale form part.

Shortly after settlement, the area in which the flat was situated was declared a housing action area. The seller had known that this was pending but had not informed the buyer. The buyer sought damages on the basis of condition 7. She argued that the words 'matter' and 'attention' were wide enough to encompass, not only repairs, but almost anything else that had been within the knowledge of the seller. **Held**: action dismissed. In the context, both of condition 7 and of surrounding conditions, it was clear that condition 7 was concerned only with repairs.

(2) Clancy v Caird (No 2) 2000 GWD 18–716 (OH)

This was an action for damages for misrepresentations (fraudulent or negligent) said to have been made by the seller of a residential care home, in particular in relation to the number of residents. After a proof, absolvitor was granted on the basis (i) that no misrepresentations had been proved, other, possibly, than statements made in good faith; (ii) that the buyer had relied mainly on other factors in making the purchase, for example the survey or the accounts; and (iii) that in any event, there was no proper basis for quantifying damages.

(3) Evans v Argus Healthcare (Glenesk) Ltd 2001 SCLR 117 (OH)

Missives were concluded for the sale of a nursing home. The seller was bound to:

> deliver, at settlement, a formal Deed of Servitude granted by the owners of the land through which the water pipe passes vouching the formal rights of the seller to use, maintain, renew and repair the said water pipe with all appropriate rights of access on all necessary occasions for purposes of maintenance, renewal and repair.

When it became apparent that a deed of servitude could not be produced for part of the route through which the pipe passed, the parties began negotiating a solution involving an *a non domino* deed backed by title insurance. Negotiations dragged on fitfully for almost two years, during which time the purchasers were running the nursing home under a separate minute of agreement. Eventually, agreement was reached on the terms of the deed, but not on the level of title insurance. When the seller finally sued for implement, the purchasers purported to rescind the contract. The seller accepted that the purchasers had a right of rescission in principle, but argued that the prolonged negotiations amounted to an implied waiver of that right. Admittedly, the fact that agreement had not been reached on all the details meant that the waiver was conditional in nature; but provided that a deed and title insurance were duly produced, the purchasers could not rescind. The purchasers argued that there had been no implied waiver. Proof before answer allowed.

As it happens, the missives contained an express provision designed to exclude implied waiver. It read:

> the rights and remedies of the Purchaser in respect of any breach of warranty, representation or undertaking shall not be affected by Completion, by any investigation made by or on behalf of the Purchaser into the affairs of the Seller, or the Business, the Purchaser failing to exercise or delay the exercise of any of its rights or remedies or any other event or matter whatsoever except a specific duly authorised waiver or release.

But the provision was held inapplicable because the obligation to produce a deed of servitude was not a 'warranty, representation or undertaking'.

Lord Macfadyen expressed dissatisfaction at the drafting:

In my view the provisions of the missives that require to be examined in order to deal with these submissions constitute a poor advertisement for the traditional process of developing the definition of the rights and obligations of seller and purchaser through qualification and counter-qualification.

(4) Gawthorpe v Stewart 2000 GWD 39–1461 (OH)

A daughter sold her house and moved in with her father. Two years later she moved out when her father refused to convey the house to her. She now sought declarator that her father had entered into an oral agreement to convey the property, and that the agreement had been set up by her subsequent actings. **Held**: there was insufficient evidence of an agreement to convey.

OPTIONS

(5) Miller Homes Ltd v Frame 2000 GWD 11–388 (OH)

Formal missives were concluded for an option to purchase. The idea was that the option would be exercised if planning permission were to be granted for residential development. Later, a question arose as to whether a valid contract had been concluded. That in turn depended on whether there was an ascertained or ascertainable price. The rule for sale contracts is that the price must either be stated, or some mechanism must be provided for its ascertainment. The mechanism must not itself require a further agreement between the parties, because in that case there could not be said to be agreement as to the price.

In the original offer the price for the option (as opposed to the price for the land itself, when the option was exercised—a separate matter with which the case was not concerned) was expressed as being:

> The purchasers shall provide free from rental, Council tax or any other recurring property tax a two-bedroomed bungalow to the value of £60,000 within the town of Hamilton. Said property shall remain in all time coming the property of the purchaser and will revert to the purchaser on the demise of both of the sellers.

To this the qualified acceptance added the further condition that the bungalow 'will be a property acceptable to them'.

It was argued for the sellers (who wished to be free of the contract) that this provision did not disclose sufficient agreement as to the price. No precise mechanism was provided for identifying the bungalow, and the requirement that the property be 'acceptable' indicated a matter on which the parties had still to reach agreement.

This argument was rejected by Lord Hamilton, for the following reasons. (i) The wording used in the missive left no room for doubt that both parties intended to enter a legally binding agreement. In those circumstances it was the court's task to try to find an agreement unless to do so would violate essential principles of the law. (ii) Applying that approach, there was sufficient specification of the mechanism for identifying a suitable bungalow. The clause identified three criteria: a two-bedroom bungalow; a maximum value; and a specified location. (iii) The requirement that the bungalow must be acceptable to the sellers merely served to narrow these criteria further by adding a fourth.

> That term thus conferred on the first defenders [the sellers] the right, exercisable in good faith, to exclude from the class of otherwise qualifying property a property which was not acceptable to them. The exercise of that right required no agreement by the pursuers.

Both the decision itself, and the approach taken in reaching it, are unexceptionable. Two points may be mentioned as of particular interest. The first is the reference to good faith. In years gone by this would have been expressed rather differently. It would have been said that, in determining what was or was not acceptable, the sellers must act reasonably and not capriciously. But here that doctrine is classified, surely correctly, as an example of the requirement of good faith. This is a sign of the times. Good faith in contract law, familiar in Continental legal systems, is making an increasing impact on the law of Scotland.

The other is a judicial aside suggesting that the rule requiring an ascertained, or ascertainable, price, although applying in sales, might not apply in options.

> It is, of course, true that agreement on the price (or a mechanism for fixing it) is a requirement for the constitution of any contract of sale. It is not, however, so evident that it is a requirement for the constitution of every option contract. Under Scots law a valid option to purchase, whether constituted as a promise or as a bilateral contract, might, I should have thought, be created without any consideration at all.

The same observation might, however, be made in relation to land itself (as opposed to an option to acquire land). Land can be sold, or it can be given away. It is not clear that the fact that consideration is not always present means that, in a case where it is present, it need not be properly specified.

LAW OF THE TENEMENT

(6) Gardner v Macneal 2000 GWD 38–1430 (IH)

This is the latest litigation about common repairs at 143–147 Bruntsfield Place, Edinburgh. The pursuer owned a flat in the tenement. A statutory notice was served requiring certain repairs to be carried out. The pursuer challenged the notice unsuccessfully. (For the successful challenge to an earlier notice, see *Gardner v City of Edinburgh Council* 1992 SLT 1149.) The other owners then arranged a common repairs scheme, with a council grant. The defender, an architect, acted as consultant to the owners. The pursuer—who apparently faced liability for a share of the repairs (on what principle is unclear: for an earlier attempt to resist payment, see *City of Edinburgh Council v Gardner* 1990 SLT 600)—sought interdict against the work being carried out, failing which an order that the work be undone. He was unsuccessful before the sheriff and again before the sheriff principal. He then appealed to the Inner House. Since by this time the work had been completed, the issue became whether the defender could be ordered to undo it. **Held**: appeal refused, on two grounds. (i) Now that the work had finished, the defender had no further connection with the property. He had no right to enter it and carry out work. In effect, the pursuer was suing the wrong party. But (ii) in any event, the crave was too unclear to be granted. A decree must leave the defender in no doubt as to what he is required to do.

This case raises some interesting questions and it is unfortunate that it could not be decided on the merits. The pursuer's main point was that the common repairs scheme went beyond the terms of the statutory notice, both in terms of the amount of work, and also the standard of repair. Under the relevant statutory provision (s 108 of the Housing (Scotland) Act 1987), it was argued, a statutory notice could only require a building to be brought up to such a standard of repair 'as is reasonable having regard to the age, character and location . . . of the house'. By contrast, a repairs grant would only be given for work with a 30-year lifespan. And since the repair went beyond the statutory notice, the pursuer could presumably not be liable for it. If the factual basis could be established, this is certainly a strong argument. But there might be other grounds for liability—for example real burdens, or, if the property in question was common property, the doctrine of necessary repair. But even these alternative grounds raise the difficult issue of standard of repair, an issue on which there is little authority.

BOUNDARY WALLS AND GABLES

(7) Newton v Godfrey (2000)
Unreported Property Cases (eds Paisley & Cusine) 86 (Sh Ct)

A common gable between two houses was in disrepair. It was accepted that the gable was owned by each party to the midpoint, but with a right of common interest in the other half. On the basis that the disrepair originated on the defender's side, the pursuer sought (i) an order requiring the defender to carry out repairs or (ii) a warrant to enter the defender's property and repair the gable himself.

The main controversy surrounded (ii). The right to have the other half-gable repaired turns on common interest. But hitherto it has appeared that common interest confers no more than a means of forcing the other owner to carry out work. The sheriff, however, was now willing to extend common interest to include a right to enter, carry out work, and recover the cost. A proof before answer was allowed.

Some aspects of this (welcome) development remain unclear. It might be thought, for example, that self-help should be allowed only where the other owner has been given a reasonable opportunity to carry out the work but has failed to do so. There may also be practical difficulties about the kind of work which needs to be carried out, and its cost.

Another feature of the case is that the pursuer was a proper liferenter. Hitherto common interest has only been pled by *owners*, but it was held that a liferenter could also found on common interest.

COMMON PROPERTY

(8) McCafferty v McCafferty 2000 SCLR 256 (Sh Ct)

In 1987 Colin McCafferty bought some heritable property. In order to avoid any possible claim from his former wife (though the details here are obscure), he took title in joint names of himself and his brother William. The disposition bore that the price was paid by both Colin and William, but it seems that only Colin put up the money. The brothers fell out and in 1997 William obtained decree in an action of division and sale. The property was duly sold and William received half of the free proceeds. In this litigation Colin sought to recover this amount on the basis of unjustified enrichment. The action failed on a number of grounds, including (i) that it had prescribed negatively, five years after the disposition; (ii) that it was incompetent to lead extrinsic evidence to contradict the statement in the disposition that both brothers had contributed to the price; and (iii) that there were no relevant averments in relation to the supposed enrichment.

Reason (ii) is of particular interest. If there are two grantees, dispositions almost always state that the price was contributed by both. This is practically a matter of style. Sometimes, though, it is not true. Solicitors should check before putting in the usual words. (Whether this was done in the present case is unclear.) Otherwise it may be difficult to contradict what is stated in the deed itself. *McCafferty* is the second case in which the courts have refused to allow extrinsic evidence to contradict the clear words of a deed. (The other is *Gordon-Rogers* v *Thomson's Exrs* 1988 SLT 618.) Probably, though, there is a way out, in the form of an application for rectification of the deed under s 8 of the Law Reform (Miscellaneous Provisions) (Scotland) Act 1985—subject, of course, to problems of proof. Rectification was not attempted in the present case. Note that a different (and apparently irreconcilable) approach to the issue of extrinsic evidence was taken in *Nottay's Tr* v *Nottay* 2000 GWD 28–1091 (case (81) below) and in *Bank of Scotland* v *Reid* 2000 GWD 22–858 (case (82) below).

(9) Mackay v Gaylor 2001 GWD 1–59 (Sh Ct)

A driveway serving two properties was owned in common. In the course of building a house on one of the properties the owner needed to use the driveway for heavy construction traffic, and also to lay pipes, cables and drains underneath. His right to do so was challenged by the owner of the other property. It appeared that the driveway had been used on previous occasions for construction traffic. The issue resolved into whether the proposed uses were 'ordinary' uses of the driveway, in which case they were permitted by the rules of common property, or 'extraordinary' uses, in which case they were not permitted. **Held**: these were ordinary uses, although this conclusion was reached with some hesitation in relation to the laying of the pipes etc.

TIMESHARES

(10) Abbott v Forest Hills Trossachs Club
Stirling Sheriff Court, 29 November 2000 (unreported)

The Abbotts had a one-week timeshare at Forest Hills. The timeshare scheme was operated by a club, of which the Abbotts were members. Executive power was in a management committee, but could be, and had been, substantially delegated to a management company. The Abbotts refused to pay a levy for the refurbishment of lodges. In retaliation they were excluded from use of the development. The Abbotts raised an action against both the club and also the management company. The current phase of litigation involved a dispute as to whether the Abbotts were entitled to sue the management company. The defenders pled, on the basis of *Foss* v *Harbottle* (1843) 2 Hare 461, that only the club could sue the management company. The contract was between the club and the company, and the Abbotts had no separate right of action. **Held**: that the Abbotts had title to sue. The effect of the contract was simply to delegate some of the club's functions to the company. The Abbotts could sue the agent as well as the principal.

For timeshares of fishing rights see **Commentary** p 112.

SERVITUDES AND RIGHTS OF WAY

(11) Bowers v Kennedy 2000 SC 555, 2000 SLT 1006 (IH)

On subdividing land, one of the plots was to become landlocked. Accordingly, an express servitude of access was reserved in the disposition of the other plot. However, it appeared (subject to proof) that that servitude had subsequently been lost by negative prescription. **Held**: notwithstanding the extinction of the express servitude, a right of access was inherent in ownership, and one would be implied. Such a right could not be extinguished by prescription. See **Commentary** p 52.

(12) Mackie v Donaldson
Hamilton Sheriff Court 31 May 2000 (unreported)

A subdivision left one of the plots landlocked. It was accepted that the landlocked plot had, by implication, a right of access over the other plot, but the extent of the right was disputed. **Held**: that in a case where the landlocked plot was undeveloped land, the normal rule would allow only a right of pedestrian access. But vehicular access would be permitted where this had been within the contemplation of the parties at the time of subdivision (*eg* because it was known that the landlocked owner was to build a garage).

For commentary on this case, see R R M Paisley, 'Property Law Update' (2000) 5 *Scottish Law & Practice Quarterly* 432 at 435.

(13) Inverness Seafield Co Ltd v Mackintosh
2001 SLT 118 (IH)

An option was entered into to buy land, or part of land. Eventually the option was exercised, but in relation to part of the land only. This left the remaining part landlocked. Accordingly, when the sellers came to adjust a disposition they sought to include an express reservation of a servitude in their favour. This was resisted by the purchasers. At first instance the Lord Ordinary accepted that an express servitude should be included, on the basis that, by necessity, a right to access was implied in the contract. See 1999 GWD 31–1497 (*Conveyancing 1999* Case (19) and p 48). On appeal that approach was rejected. Following *Bowers* v *Kennedy* 2000 SC 555, 2000 SLT 1006, it was said that a right of access arising from necessity was different from a servitude. Hence, to allow an express servitude in the disposition was to give something other than that which would be implied by law. See **Commentary** p 54.

(14) Class 98 Ltd v Hogg 2001 GWD 1–61 (OH)

The pursuers were constructing an access road to Larbert High School as part of a PFI agreement. This required cutting across an existing road (Carrongrange Avenue) and, for that purpose, removing parts of a wall and a boundary hedge, and the construction of three separate junctions. At the point of intersection, the existing road was the property of the defenders, but the pursuers had a servitude for pedestrian and vehicular access. The defenders were opposed to the new access road, and, at a time when the road was almost complete, placed building blocks, metal containers and other obstacles on their property to prevent its completion. The pursuers sought a declarator as to their rights to use the existing road, and interim orders for interdict and removal of the obstructions. The present stage of litigation was concerned only with the interim orders.

The pursuers faced two potential difficulties. First, instead of using the strip, along which servitude rights were held, from end to end, their plan required that they cut across the strip. And second, their plan involved a substantial amount of construction on the servient tenement. **Held**: interim orders granted, having regard to the balance of convenience, although without prejudice to the possibility that the pursuers might ultimately be held to have exceeded their rights under the servitude. In relation to the first difficulty, the words of the servitude ('right of access . . . over and across' the strip) were helpful to the pursuers' case. In relation to the second:

> [h]ow far the pursuers may go in constructing new junctions, and altering existing walls and hedges, is . . . a matter of some difficulty that cannot properly be resolved at this stage. I do not consider that the rule against damaging the servient tenement necessarily precludes opening gaps in hedges and walls, where that is necessary if the right of access is to be effectively enjoyed.

(15) North East District Council v Nisbet 2000 SCLR 413 (IH)

In this case a local authority was successful in vindicating a public right of way. It was proved that the way had been used by pedestrians for its full length for at least 40 years prior to the 1920s; and that while it had been little used since then, the use had not been so slight as to allow the way to be lost by negative prescription. The interest of the case lies in (i) the kind of evidence that is sufficient to establish possession 80 years ago, and (ii) the view taken by the Lord Coulsfield (p 417E–F) that

> 'once a right of way is established, it can only be lost by proof of non-use for the prescriptive period, so that very much less in the way of use may suffice to maintain a right of way in existence than is necessary for its creation. In the course of argument there was discussion of various circumstances in which it might be said that continuing use was so small as to be immaterial (such as the case of a poacher using the route by night), but we do not think it necessary to discuss such extreme cases. The general rule appears to be that continuing use which is not, in all the circumstances, negligible or immaterial will suffice to maintain the right'.

(16) MacKinnon v Argyll and Bute Council 2000 GWD 11–371 (OH)

A local authority adopted a way, at Ganavan near Oban, as a public road. The way, and surrounding land, were partly owned and partly leased (from the authority) by Mr MacKinnon. Since adoption would probably mean public access, Mr MacKinnon challenged the authority's decision to adopt on a number of grounds, including (i) that the way was not a road in respect that there was a public right of passage, and (ii) that the power of a roads authority was excluded by s 151(3)(c) of the Roads (Scotland) Act 1984 in respect of land owned or managed by a local authority for recreational purposes. The challenge was upheld, and the entry on the list of public roads reduced. See **Commentary** p 49.

(17) Elmford Ltd v City of Glasgow Council (No 2) 2001 SC 267 (OH)

A council acquired land, under compulsory procedures, for the purposes of constructing a road. The road was duly constructed. Only part of the land was metalled, so that there was a substantial unmetalled strip on either side. A developer, who owned adjacent land, asserted the right, as a member of the public, to use the strip to reach the road. This right was disputed by the Council. **Held**: that, on the facts, the strip was not part of the road and could not be used by the developer. See **Commentary** p 51.

REAL BURDENS

(18) Grampian Joint Police Board v Pearson 2001 SLT 90 (OH)

Land was feued subject to a reversion at the option of the superior on the occurrence of certain events. The amount to be paid by the superior was not to exceed 'the original cost of the said buildings'. This clause was **held** to be void from uncertainty. See **Commentary** p 74.

(19) Dumbarton District Council v McLaughlin 2000 HousLR 16 (Sh Ct)

Circumstances in which a purported real burden to pay factoring charges to a local authority was held to be unenforceable. See **Commentary** p 72–74.

(20) Massey v Paterson 2000 GWD 35–1342 (Sh Ct)

In a housing estate a deed of conditions prohibited the parking of caravans. The owner of each house had enforcement rights under the deed. When the prohibition was breached by the defender, no immediate action was taken by the pursuer, who lived opposite, because he did not know about the deed of conditions. When, later, he attempted to enforce the prohibition, the defender argued that he must be taken to have acquiesced in the breach. This defence was rejected on the basis (i) that the pursuer objected as soon as he learned of the deed of conditions, and (ii) that in any case, there was no prejudice to the defender from the delay.

PASSING OF PROPERTY

(21) Burnett's Tr v Grainger 2000 SLT (Sh Ct) 116

A sale transaction settled on 8 November 1990, but the purchasers' disposition was not recorded until 27 January 1992. By that time the seller had been sequestrated, and title completed by her trustee by means of a recorded notice of title. The trustee sought declarator that the property had vested in him, and warrant for the eviction of the purchasers. **Held**: action dismissed. Following *Sharp* v *Thomson* 1997 SC(HL) 66, the seller ceased to have a beneficial interest in the property once the disposition had been delivered and the price paid. Accordingly, the property did not fall within the sequestration. See **Commentary** p 93.

EXECUTION OF DEEDS

(22) Russo v Hardey 2000 GWD 27–1049 (IH)

This was an action of reduction on grounds of force and fear. The pursuer had executed a probative writ obliging her to give certain heritable property to her son. After proof it was held that the pursuer had been intimidated by her son's threatening behaviour. In that context it was irrelevant that the pursuer may have owed her son money, because she was not obliged to fulfil that obligation by conveying the property in question. (See 1997 GWD 6–246.) The son reclaimed, arguing a substantial number of points in relation to the detailed evidence. The reclaiming motion was refused.

PROPERTY ENQUIRY CERTIFICATES

(23) National Children's Home and Orphanage Trs v Stirrat Park Hogg
2000 GWD 35–1329 (OH)

The pursuers took on a full repairing and insuring lease in reliance on a property inquiry certificate provided by the defenders. It turned out that the certificate had failed to pick up a statutory notice. The pursuers' share of the repairs was £28,574. They sued for damages. The present report is concerned with a dispute over the basis of the action. The pursuers could have sued in negligence. However, they appear to have sued instead on the basis of breach of an express warranty. But while this avoided the need to show negligence, it was **held** that it had the effect of importing the limitations on liability which were contained in the warranty.

(24) Maypark Properties Ltd v Stirrat 2000 GWD 37–1412 (Sh Ct)

A second case in which those providing a property enquiry certificate failed to pick up a statutory notice. Again purchasers acquired property in reliance on the certificate, and again they sued for damages. The action was raised in delict, presumably on the basis that the certificate was instructed by, and hence the contract was with, the seller. In fact, no damages were held to be due, because it was not shown that the purchasers paid more for the property than it was actually worth. But in the course of his judgment the sheriff principal expressed the view: (i) that, although the certificate was instructed by the seller, the searcher was in sufficient proximity to a purchaser to give rise to a duty of care; (ii) that it made no difference for this purpose that the pursuers were not the same as the person with whom missives were concluded but were nominees of that person; and (iii) that since a searcher collated information rather than offered expert advice, liability would be established merely by showing a failure to exercise reasonable care.

REGISTRATION OF TITLE

(25) Keeper of the Registers of Scotland v M R S Hamilton Ltd
2000 SC 271, 2000 SLT 352 (IH)

On first registration of titles relating to some ultra-long leases the Keeper had omitted leasehold casualties. M R S Hamilton Ltd, who were now the landlords, sued for indemnity for their loss. They had not been landlords at first registration but they held assignations of the claim from the then landlords. Before the Lands Tribunal (19 May 1998, unreported) the claim was admitted in principle and a proof allowed as to quantum. The Keeper appealed on two points.

    The first was whether rectification was retrospective. M R S Hamilton Ltd were entitled only to be put into the position they would have been in had rectification been allowed. But if rectification was not retrospective, they would have had no entitlement to casualty payments arising before the date on which rectification was refused. It was held that rectification was not retrospective.

That confirms the view taken in *Stevenson-Hamilton's Exrs* v *McStay* 1999 SLT 1175 (*Conveyancing 1999* Case (32) and p 68).

The second was whether s 12(1)(d) of the Land Registration (Scotland) Act 1979 (indemnity in respect of an error or omission in the land certificate) referred to (i) *any* error in the land certificate (which would include errors also present in the title sheet) or (ii) only discrepancies between the land certificate and the title sheet. The Lands Tribunal had favoured (i), as had Lord Hamilton in *M R S Hamilton* v *Keeper of the Registers of Scotland (No 1)* 1999 SLT 829. But the First Division found (ii) to be correct. On this point see **Commentary** p 111.

(26) Kaur v Singh (No 2) 2000 SLT 1323, 2000 SCLR 944 (IH)

This is the successor to *Kaur* v *Singh* 1999 SC 180, 1998 SCLR. The pursuer co-owned a flat with her husband at 3/2, 30 Woodlands Drive, Glasgow. Her husband sold it without telling her, forging her signature. Mr Singh, the purchaser, was entered on the Register as owner, but—since the signature was forged—the Register was inaccurate as to the half share which had belonged to the pursuer. At one stage the pursuer's strategy seems to have been to dispossess Mr Singh by force, so that he was no longer a 'proprietor in possession'. Latterly this approach was abandoned, and the pursuer accepted that the Keeper could not rectify the Register against Mr Singh. Instead she sought payment of indemnity.

In this, presumably final, stage of the litigation, it was accepted that indemnity was due; and it was also accepted that the pursuer's loss was to be measured as at 8 March 1996 (the date that the inaccurate entry was made), although the court reserved its view on this point (at 1328K). (A more plausible date is the date on which rectification was refused: see the previous case.) The dispute was now about quantum. As at 8 March 1996 the flat was valued at £51,000. But until 7 March it had been subject to a secured loan, with the Woolwich, of £41,000. So the pursuer's share of the equity was only £5,000. The pursuer's husband had redeemed the loan as part of the fraudulent sale.

The pursuer claimed £25,500 (*ie* half the value of the flat). The Keeper was willing to pay only £5,000, on the basis that that was the real loss from the total transaction. At first instance Lord Macfadyen had preferred the argument for the pursuer: see 2000 SLT 1324, 2000 SCLR 187, 1999 HousLR 76 (*Conveyancing 1999* Case (34)). This view was now affirmed by the Inner House. The broader circumstances were not regarded as relevant.

> In considering what loss was suffered by the pursuer 'as a result of' the Keeper's refusal to make rectification, we can see no basis for going back beyond the inaccuracy, and beyond the repayment of the debt to the Woolwich, to a situation of indebtedness which, for whatever reason, had been brought to an end before any alteration in the pursuer's interest as it appeared on the register (p 1329F).

If the Keeper had duly rectified, the pursuer would have received an unencumbered half share of the flat, worth £25,500. That, therefore, was the extent of her loss for present purposes.

The result looks like a windfall gain for the pursuer. In theory, Mr Kaur might claim from Mrs Kaur one half of the loan of £41,000, which he had paid off to her benefit. If that were to happen, Mrs Kaur would end up with £25,500 − £20,500 = £5,000. But one suspects that in practice she will end up keeping the extra.

(27) Stevenson-Hamilton's Exrs v McStay (No 2) 2000 GWD 22–872 (OH)

In 1983 Mr McStay granted an *a non domino* disposition to Mrs McStay of a gap site at 81 Clyde Street, Carluke, belonging to Stevenson-Hamilton's executors. The disposition was recorded in the Register of Sasines. In 1993 Mrs McStay conveyed to herself and her husband and applied for registration in the Land Register. The McStays were duly registered without exclusion of indemnity. The executors then raised an action for reduction of the dispositions, and rectification of the Register. **Held**: both reduction and rectification granted. In relation to the latter the McStays had been fraudulent, or at least careless, in their responses to questions, including the question about peaceable possession, in the form 1 application. Hence, there could be rectification against them. See **Commentary** p 109.

[Another aspect of this case is digested at (68).]

RIGHT-TO-BUY LEGISLATION

(28) Ross v City of Dundee Council
2000 SLT (Lands Tr) 2, 2000 HousLR 84

A tenant applied to purchase. The landlords did not respond within the one-month deadline. The tenant then applied to the Lands Tribunal, but she died before a decision could be reached. Her executor sought to continue the action. **Held**: that upon the tenant's death the secure tenancy ceased to exist and that accordingly any right to buy which there may have been had disappeared.

(29) Graham v Northern Joint Police Board
2000 SLT (Lands Tr) 7, 2000 HousLR 74

A tenant applied to purchase in 1996. There was no response but it was not until 1999 that the tenant applied to the Lands Tribunal. The landlords argued that any right to buy which there may have been had been impliedly waived. **Held**: that the tenant's delay was understandable in the particular circumstances of the case, that there was therefore no implied waiver, and that he was entitled to proceed.

(30) Higgins v North Lanarkshire Council 2000 GWD 31–1236 (Lands Tr)

A tenant applied to buy. Part of the property had already been conveyed by the Council to his neighbour, also under the right-to-buy legislation. See **Commentary** pp 105 and 110.

(31) Lock v City of Edinburgh Council 2000 GWD 31–1237 (Lands Tr)

Section 61(2)(c) of the Housing (Scotland) Act 1987 requires a secure tenant to have two years of occupation before the right to buy emerges. This was a case of a tenant who had occupied various council properties over several years but with substantial breaks. **Held**: that the requirements of s 61(2)(c) had not been satisfied.

(32) Scherrer v Dumfries & Galloway Council 2000 HousLR 42

Schedule 2 para 6 to the Housing (Scotland) Act 1987 states that a tenancy is not a secure tenancy if it 'consists of or includes premises which are used' for stated commercial purposes. Circumstances in which it was held that this provision applied, with the result that there was no right to buy.

LEASES

(33) Highland and Universal Properties Ltd v Safeway Properties Ltd
2000 SC 297, 2000 SLT 414 (IH)

An important decision on the enforceability of 'keep open' clauses in commercial leases. See **Commentary** p 67.

(34) Optical Express (Gyle) Ltd v Marks & Spencer plc 2000 SLT 644 (OH)

When Optical Express took a unit in a shopping centre they insisted that the landlords agree to limit the number of opticians trading in the centre. The original landlords having sold on, the question arose as to whether this agreement was enforceable against singular successors. See **Commentary** p 56.

(35) P & O Property Holdings Ltd v City of Glasgow Council
2000 SLT 444 (OH)

In 1982 Zip Properties Ltd granted a 20-year lease to Pars Bakery Ltd (later called Starpro Ltd) of a shop at 59 Kinfauns Drive, Drumchapel, part of the Drumchapel Shopping Centre. Zip themselves held on a long lease so this was a sub-lease. In March 1997 Pars went into liquidation. The liquidator handed back the keys to the landlords, who by this time were P & O Property Holdings. Thereafter the shop stood empty. The landlords had agreed to relet to Victoria Wine but it seems that at the time of the litigation there was still no contract. The lease contained the usual irritancy clause, but the landlords did not seek to invoke it, nor did they accept the liquidator's repudiation. Pars had not yet been dissolved.

The local authority issued rates notices to the landlords, but the latter denied liability. Section 154 of the Local Government (Scotland) Act 1994 provides that where property is unoccupied then 'a person entitled to possession' is liable

only for reduced rates. Were the landlords 'a person entitled to possession'?
Held: subject to proof of the landlords' averments that they had neither irritated
nor accepted the liquidator's repudiation, that they were not.

At common law both landlord and tenant have possession, the landlord having
civil (indirect) possession, and the tenant natural (direct) possession. The statement
by the Lord Ordinary (Macfadyen) that 'an ordinary incident of a lease is that
during its subsistence entitlement to possession of the subjects of the lease rests
with the tenant to the exclusion of the landlord' must therefore be taken as referring
only to natural possession, and presumably the word is being used in the same
sense in the statute. But the further statement that 'once . . . the tenant ceases to
exist, entitlement to possession reverts to the landlord' might perhaps be
questioned, in the light of s 654 of the Companies Act 1985.

(36) Minevco Ltd v Barratt Southern Ltd 2000 SLT 790 (IH)

Landlords raised an action against their tenants seeking declarator that the latter
were in breach of their obligations under a lease of property at Schoolhill, Aberdeen,
and for an order requiring them to erect certain buildings, which failing to pay
damages of £1,500,000. The Lord Ordinary allowed proof before answer: see
1999 GWD 5–266 (*Conveyancing 1999* Case (41)). The tenants reclaimed, but
unsuccessfully. The case is a fact-specific one.

(37) Trustees of the West Errol Trust v Lawrie 2000 SLT 911 (IH)

James Lawrie was an agricultural tenant at Clashbenny, Glencarse, having inherited
the farm from his father. When he was sequestrated, the landlords served a notice
to quit. This was based on s 22(2)(f) of the Agricultural Holdings (Scotland) Act
1991 which makes apparent insolvency a ground for termination. The landlords
raised an action to remove him. His defence was that the landlords had waived
their rights, by agreeing to a new rent. This defence went to arbitration and was
rejected. A case was stated to the sheriff, and when that was unsuccessful the
tenant appealed to the Inner House, again unsuccessfully. Finally, decree was
pronounced. Curiously, the final stage was reported first, at 1999 SCLR 624
(*Conveyancing 1999* Case (47)). The present report covers the earlier stage of the
case stated and subsequent appeal to the Inner House.

(38) Creston Land and Estates plc v Brown 2000 SC 320 (OH)

The pursuers raised an ordinary action in the sheriff court seeking (i) declarator
of their rights and (ii) ejection. The action was subsequently remitted to the Court
of Session. The defenders used land as a riding centre, and argued that they had
an agricultural tenancy under the Agricultural Holdings (Scotland) Act 1991.
The pursuers claimed that there was no lease at all, but merely a licence to occupy
which had now come to an end. The reported case is concerned not with the
substance of the dispute but with procedure. Section 35(1) of the Sheriff Courts
(Scotland) Act 1970 provides that actions *ad factum praestandum* and actions for

the recovery of possession of heritable property can proceed *only* as summary causes. The question here was whether the declaratory crave had a real purpose or not, the defender's argument being that in the latter case the declaratory crave should not be allowed to circumvent the statutory provisions. **Held**: following *Milmor Properties Ltd* v *W & T Investment Co Ltd* 2000 SLT (Sh Ct) 2 (digested at (70) below), that the declaratory crave had a real function and that the action could therefore proceed. It was observed that a declaratory crave is never competent in a summary cause.

(39) Bannerman Co Ltd v Cromarty Firth Port Authority 2000 GWD 11–400 (Sh Ct)

B granted a short lease to C of three berths on a pier. C refused to pay the rent on the ground that the pier had become unsafe. B sued. The question was whether the obligation of repair rested on the landlord or the tenant. **Held**: that on a proper construction of the lease it rested on the tenant, and decree granted.

(40) Knapdale (Nominees) Ltd v Donald 2000 SCLR 1013 (OH)

A farmer was a tenant. In due course he took his sons into partnership. Later he died. The landlords argued that the farmer had impliedly renounced the lease, that a new lease had *de facto* arisen in favour of the firm, and that on the dissolution of the firm upon his death the lease came to an end. See **Commentary** p 62.

(41) Euro Properties Scotland Ltd v Alam 2000 GWD 23–896 (OH)

This case turned on the enforceability of an irritancy in a commercial lease in the light of the provisions of the Law Reform (Miscellaneous Provisions) (Scotland) Act 1985. See **Commentary** p 66.

(42) Age Ltd v Brown 2000 GWD 27–1018 (OH)

The defender was an expert who had set the rent pursuant to a rent review clause. The tenant sought to reduce the defender's determination of the rent. The relevancy of the action depended on whether the defender had acted as an arbiter or as an independent expert. **Held**: that he had acted as an independent expert, and action dismissed.

(43) Sproat v South West Services (Galloway) Ltd 2000 GWD 37–1416 (OH)

On the death, intestate, of the lessee of a non-assignable lease, s 16 of the Succession (Scotland) Act 1964 comes into play. This case concerns the interpretation of that section, and illustrates a pitfall for practitioners. See **Commentary** p 64.

(44) Waydale Ltd v DHL Holdings (UK) Ltd (No 2) 2001 SLT 224 (OH)

Commercial property was let. The landlords insisted that the parent company of the tenants should guarantee due payment of the rent. The question in dispute was whether this guarantee was enforceable against the parent company by a singular successor of the landlord. See **Commentary** p 60.

(45) Sears Properties Netherlands BV v Coal Pension Properties Ltd 2000 SCLR 1002 (OH)

A sub-lease provided that any assignation had to be consented to both by the mid-landlord and by the head landlord. **Held**: that, as a contract between two other parties, it conferred no rights on a third (the head landlord). Accordingly, the head landlord could not prevent an assignation of the sub-lease. See **Commentary** p 69.

(46) Buchan v North Lanarkshire Council 2000 HousLR 98 (Sh Ct)

A significant new case on the long-running issue of landlord liability for dampness.

(47) Morgan v Morgan and Kyle & Carrick District Council 2000 HousLR 90 (Sh Ct)

This was decided in 1984 but is reported for the first time only now. A local authority obtained decree for recovery of possession. The tenant's wife then raised an action for declarator that her occupancy rights under the Matrimonial Homes (Family Protection) (Scotland) Act 1981 were unaffected by the decree against her husband, and also seeking transfer of the tenancy to her name conform to s 13 of the 1981 Act. The action was dismissed. The termination of the tenancy was not a 'dealing' by the husband and hence the provisions of the Act protecting occupancy rights against 'dealings' could give the pursuer no assistance. The case is remarkable for the fact that the only cases cited were from 1550 and 1630 (*Wallace* v *Cathcart* (1550) Balfour's *Practicks* II, 461 and *Rowallan* v *Boyd* (1630) Mor 13825).

(48) MacLeod v Alexander 2000 HousLR 136 (Sh Ct)

The subjects of let had a badly leaking roof. When the landlord failed to carry out adequate repairs, the tenant withheld the payment of all rent. The landlord sued for rent. **Held**: that, since the subjects were not habitable, the tenant was entitled to withhold the rent, but decree granted in respect of certain arrears.

(49) Little v Irving (2000) *Unreported Property Cases* (eds Paisley & Cusine) 120 (Sh Ct)

Two neighbouring tenants held on ultra-long leases. The defenders' property included a lane which gave access from the street to the rear of the house. For more than 20 years this lane had been used by the pursuers and their predecessors for access to their property. When the defenders withdrew access, the pursuers sought interdict.

If the properties had been owned, rather than held on the quasi-ownership constituted by an ultra-long lease, the dispute would have been easily disposed of. After 20 years a servitude would have been established by positive prescription. But a servitude requires two properties in separate ownership. In the present case the owner (*ie* the landlord) was the same. It is probably the law that there is some equivalent to a servitude in a question between tenants (or indeed between tenant and landlord in relation to land still occupied by the landlord); and, if so, such a right may be constituted by express grant in the lease. But it cannot be constituted by prescription, because the relevant provision in the Prescription and Limitation (Scotland) Act 1973 (s 3) is confined to 'servitudes'. In the present case, there was no express grant, only possession. Accordingly, there was no clear basis for arguing that the pursuers had a right to use the defenders' lane.

Faced with this difficulty, the pursuers chose a novel approach. A person who can show a *prima facie* title followed by seven years' possession is entitled to retain that possession unless or until a better title can be shown. This is a so-called possessory judgment, once fashionable but now superseded by better remedies. Its attraction in the present case was that it might be available without too careful an inquiry into the pursuers' rights. Recent assignations of the lease had included an express right of access. That might—just—qualify as a *prima facie* title. If so, the possession would do the rest.

In the event, the sheriff (M J Fletcher) was satisfied that the requirements of a possessory judgment had been met and granted interdict accordingly. The value of the victory seems questionable, however. Unless the pursuers are able to show a proper right, the defenders will be able to raise an action based on their lease and have the pursuers interdicted in turn. Ultimate victory will thus be theirs. This suggests the 'futility of the remedy' of a possessory judgment (in the sheriff's words, at p 135) in a case where ultimate right is not with the pursuer.

STANDARD SECURITIES AND FLOATING CHARGES

(50) Broadway v Clydesdale Bank plc 2000 GWD 19–763 (OH)

This case, like the next four, deals with the question of whether a standard security can be set aside on the ground of the alleged bad faith of the lender under the doctrine established in *Smith v Bank of Scotland* 1997 SC (HL) 111. See **Commentary** p 87.

(51) Royal Bank of Scotland plc v Clark
2000 SLT (Sh Ct) 101, 2000 SCLR 193 (Sh Ct)

This case, like the previous case and the next three, deals with the question of whether a standard security can be set aside on the ground of the alleged bad faith of the lender under the doctrine established in *Smith* v *Bank of Scotland* 1997 SC (HL) 111. See **Commentary** p 88.

(52) Wright v Cotias Investments Inc 2000 SCLR 324, 2001 SLT 353 (OH)

This, like the previous two and the next two cases, deals with the question of whether a standard security can be set aside on the ground of the alleged bad faith of the lender under the doctrine established in *Smith* v *Bank of Scotland* 1997 SC (HL) 111. See **Commentary** p 89.

(53) Royal Bank of Scotland plc v Wilson 2001 SLT (Sh Ct) 2

This, like the previous three cases, and the next case, deals with the question of whether a standard security can be set aside on the ground of the alleged bad faith of the lender under the doctrine established in *Smith* v *Bank of Scotland* 1997 SC (HL) 111. See **Commentary** p 89.

(54) Ahmed v Clydesdale Bank plc 2001 SLT 423 (OH)

This case, like the previous four cases, deals with the question of whether a standard security can be set aside on the ground of the alleged bad faith of the lender under the doctrine established in *Smith* v *Bank of Scotland* 1997 SC (HL) 111. See **Commentary** p 89.

(55) Bank of Ireland v Morton 2000 GWD 14–522 (Sh Ct)

The Bank of Ireland lent £250,000 to Lewis Lloyd Holdings Ltd. Brian Morton, the managing director, guaranteed the loan. The company granted to the bank a standard security over property known as Hazelburn Business Centre in Campbeltown. The company later went into receivership. It turned out that the Bank of Ireland's standard security was ranked after two floating charges, in favour of the Royal Bank of Scotland and Bass Brewers. Had the standard security been ranked first the loan would, averred the defender, have been repaid in full. When the Bank of Ireland sued Mr Morton for the shortfall, he pled that they had been under a duty to procure a first-ranked security. **Held**: that the defence was relevantly pled.

The opinion issued by Sheriff Principal McInnes is a valuable one. Mention should be made of his observation that 'in the construction of commercial contracts courts now tend to pay somewhat less attention to linguistic considerations and more to the factual background which led to the contract being entered into than once they did'.

This sort of issue can arise very easily. Ideally, the point will be covered, one way or the other, in the documentation.

[This is related to the case that follows.]

(56) Bank of Ireland v Bass Brewers Ltd 2000 GWD 28–1077 (OH)

This litigation follows on from *Griffith and Powdrill (Receivers of Lewis Lloyd Holdings Ltd) Petrs* 1998 GWD 40–2037, and is also related to the previous case. Though in form an action for rectification under s 8 of the Law Reform (Miscellaneous Provisions) (Scotland) Act 1985, in substance this was a case about the mutual priority between a standard security and a floating charge. See **Commentary** p 81.

[Another aspect of this case is digested at (74).]

(57) Grantly Developments v Clydesdale Bank plc 2000 GWD 6–213 (OH)

Debtors in a standard security sought interim interdict against enforcement on the ground of alleged breach of contract by the creditors. Refused, since no *prima facie* case had been stated. This is an earlier, and related, action to *Clydesdale Bank plc v Grantly Developments* 2000 SLT 1369 (digested at (79) below).

NEGLIGENT SURVEYS

(58) Purdie v Dryburgh 2000 SC 497 (IH)

David and Isobel Purdie owned a plot of land in Musselburgh and wanted to build a house on it. They retained the defender to advise on the foundations. He said that 'nominally reinforced strip footings' would be sufficient. In fact, the more expensive system of concrete pilings proved necessary. The Purdies sued for the additional cost. While admitting negligence, the defender argued that he should not be liable for the whole additional cost, since the Purdies were going to have to pay for concrete pilings anyway. **Held**: that he was liable for the full cost, because if the Purdies had known the true position they would not have proceeded with the project.

(59) Douglas v Stuart Wise Ogilvie Estates Ltd 2000 GWD 25–953 (OH)

A couple bought a house which, they said, turned out to be affected by damp and rot. They sued (i) the estate agents for not having disclosed the full details of a survey, (ii) their solicitors for having failed to ensure that they knew what was in the survey, for having failed to inform them of the conditions that were being attached to the loan, and for having failed to insert an appropriate clause in the offer, and (iii) a firm of timber specialists for not having carried out a proper inspection. Proof before answer allowed. The main issue was assessment of quantum. It was observed that the normal measure of loss in such a case is the difference between the price paid and the value, but the alternative measure of repair costs can also be appropriate and that the decision between the two could appropriately be taken after proof. Certain heads of claim were disallowed as being too remote. The claim based on the terms of the offer was disallowed on a pleading point.

SOLICITORS AND ESTATE AGENTS

(60) Ross Harper & Murphy v Banks
2000 SC 500, 2000 SLT 699, 2000 SCLR 736 (OH)

This case has sent shockwaves through the legal profession. Though it is not in its essence a conveyancing case, it arose out of a conveyancing problem. Northern Rock Building Society retained Messrs Ross Harper & Murphy to take a standard security for them. The title contained a burden conferring on the sellers a conditional right of pre-emption at a specified price. Messrs Ross Harper & Murphy did not report this to the building society. In the event the debtor defaulted, and when the building society enforced their security the pre-emption holders exercised their pre-emption right. The result was that the building society suffered a loss. They successfully sued Messrs Ross Harper & Murphy on the ground that the burden was of a kind which should have been reported to the lender. Messrs Ross Harper & Murphy thereupon sued the solicitor who acted, who by this time was no longer a partner. **Held**: that the action was relevant.

The case illustrates the importance of alerting lenders to burdens which may have a significant impact on the value of the security. More broadly, it has led to partners checking, and revising, the terms of their partnership deeds.

(61) Paul v Ogilvy 2001 SLT 171 (OH)

A solicitor overlooked the provisions of s 16 of the Succession (Scotland) Act about what is to happen to a lease on the death of the tenant. As a result the lease was forfeited and the tenant claimed damages. See **Commentary** p 117.

(62) Leeds & Holbeck Building Society v Alex Morison & Co
2001 SCLR 41 (OH)

When debtors defaulted, the heritable creditors sold the property, but there was a shortfall, and they sued their solicitors for having failed to disclose certain information. Had they known this information, the creditors argued, they would not have made the loan in the first place. See **Commentary** p 114.

(63) Cheltenham & Gloucester Building Society v
Royal & Sun Alliance Insurance
2000 GWD 32–1253 (OH)

Lenders suffered loss as a result of the fault of the solicitor whom they had retained. The solicitor being bankrupt, they sued his insurers direct, under the Third Parties (Rights against Insurers) Act 1930. The latter denied liability on the basis that the Master Policy covered only cases where a solicitor acted in good faith, whereas in this case he had (averred the defenders) not acted in good faith. Proof before answer allowed. See **Commentary** p 116.

BOUNDARY DISPUTES/PRESCRIPTION

(64) Young v West 2000 GWD 7–262 (Sh Ct)

This was a fact-specific case involving a boundary dispute between two neighbours. The titles were clear, but could not be properly worked out on the ground because of the disappearance of one of the original boundary features (the abutment of a railway bridge). Proof before answer.

(65) Summers v Crichton 2000 GWD 40–1495 (OH)

This was a dispute between neighbours over ownership of a piece of land on which the defender had built a wall. Both parties derived their title from the Crown Estate Commissioners in the 1970s, but the title of the defender was now on the Land Register. After a proof it was **held** that the pursuers had failed to demonstrate that the disputed property was theirs.

The decision contains several matters of interest.

(1) The defender argued that, since her title was now on the Land Register, the boundaries were as shown on the title sheet, and these necessarily superseded any title of the pursuers held on the Sasine Register. Surprisingly, this argument was rejected. See **Commentary** p 107.

(2) The defender argued that, while her break-off grant in the 1970s was the later of the two, the title could none the less form the basis of prescriptive acquisition, even assuming that the earlier deed in favour of the pursuers had conveyed the disputed area. This argument too was rejected. According to Lord Cameron of Lochbroom (para 39):

> While it is no objection that such a title flows *a non domino*, that title must still be such as to comprehend the area in dispute. In the present case, it would require the court to presume that the Crown Commissioners had intended to derogate, or by oversight had derogated, from the original disposition to Mr Millar [the pursuers' predecessor] . . . I can find no reason to consider that they did so.

This introduces a subjective element into prescriptive writs which is both novel and, in context, out of place. The question is not what the granters intended but whether it is a *possible* reading of the words actually used that the disputed property is included. For this purpose it is not legitimate to have recourse to earlier deeds (such as the deed by which the Commissioners may have conveyed the property to Mr Millar). See D Johnston, *Prescription and Limitation* (1999) paras 15.26 to 15.28.

(3) Much evidence was led as to whether the pursuers could be regarded as having acquiesced in the building of the wall. In the end the evidence was deemed insufficient—and, of course, unnecessary in view of the eventual conclusion that there had been no encroachment.

(4) Finally, the Lord Ordinary indicated that, had encroachment been established, he would have awarded damages (of £2000) rather than order demolition. This confirms the modern trend whereby courts are reluctant to order the demolition, even though the building encroaches on the property of a neighbour.

(66) Patterson v Menzies 2001 GWD 1–5 (OH)

This was a dispute between neighbours over the ownership of certain land. The land might belong to the pursuer, on the basis of an *a non domino* conveyance followed by possession for ten years; or it might belong to the defender by virtue of a title granted in the 1920s; or it might belong to neither. The pursuer had obtained an interim interdict *ex parte* to prevent the defender from removing trees or otherwise encroaching on the disputed land. The defender now sought recall. **Held**: until the title dispute could be resolved, the status quo should be retained. That meant that the defender should not be allowed to innovate on the possession. Recall was refused.

(67) Hoggan's Curator ad Litem v Cowan
2000 GWD 27–1050 (Sh Ct)

The boundary between two, former council, houses was disputed. In each case the conveyance from the Council was *habile* to include the ground in dispute, but in neither case had the ten years necessary for positive prescription elapsed. Thus, while the history of possession was established by proof (albeit with difficulty), the possession was found not to be conclusive of ownership.

(68) Stevenson-Hamilton's Exrs v McStay (No 2)
2000 GWD 22–872 (OH)

There was an *a non domino* disposition of a gap site, duly recorded, in favour of the defenders. This was followed by very occasional acts of possession, by the defenders, such as clearing rubbish, trimming hedges and cutting grass. In the same period the original owners (the pursuers) had dug some trial pits using a JCB excavator and had made applications for planning permission. **Held**: after a proof, that there was insufficient possession for the site to be acquired by positive prescription. 'There was nothing done by the defenders in my opinion, which would indicate to a reasonably observant owner that someone was trying to occupy his property and so found a prescriptive title.'

[Another aspect of this case is digested at (27).]

(69) Caledonian Heritable Ltd v Canyon Investments Ltd
2001 GWD 1–62 (OH)

This case raises, but without at this stage deciding, the issue of whether acquiescence in encroachment is capable of binding successors. The pursuers and the defenders were neighbours in Hope Street, Edinburgh. In 1983 predecessors of the defenders built a fire escape in such a way that its final section rested on the backyard of the pursuers' property. The pursuers raised an action for it to be removed. Presumably at the time when it was first erected, the fire escape was acquiesced in by the pursuers' authors. The defenders argued that the pursuers in turn were personally barred. The argument proceeded both on acquiescence to encroachment and also, in the alternative, on the basis of a servitude right having been created by encroachment. Both versions encountered the difficulty as to whether a successor could be bound by acquiescence. The defenders founded on a well-known statement in Gloag on *Contract* (2nd edn p 170) that, while successors are not generally bound, they may be if either (i) they have notice of the encroachment or (ii) if the encroachment is obvious. But the difficulty, as the pursuers pointed out, is that the cases cited by Gloag are not concerned with encroachment.

By allowing a proof before answer, Lady Cosgrove indicated that she accepted the possibility, to put it no stronger, that there might be exceptions to the rule that successors are not bound:

> I consider that issues of fact such as the character and cost of the staircase and the circumstances surrounding its construction on the pursuers' land in 1983 require to be resolved before a decision can properly be reached as to whether sufficient specialities exist to take the case outwith the ambit of the general rule.

Another issue to be considered at the proof is whether the court should exercise its discretion to refuse an order of removal, substituting instead an award of damages.

(70) Milmor Properties Ltd v W & T Investment Co Ltd
2000 SLT (Sh Ct) 2

Section 35(1) of the Sheriff Courts (Scotland) Act 1971 provides (strangely) that actions *ad factum praestandum* and actions for the recovery of possession of heritable property can proceed *only* as summary causes. In practice this rule is often outflanked by adding a crave for declarator, which brings the action back within the OCR. In the present case there was a boundary dispute, and one owner raised an action seeking declarator that the disputed area belonged to them and also seeking an order requiring the defenders to remove certain structures. The defenders had pleas to the merits, but also argued that the action was incompetent as an ordinary cause. **Held**: that the action was competent. The real question was not the technical one of the craves but the substantial one of the nature of the action. The crave for declarator had a real function and the action could therefore proceed.

The decision was followed in *Creston Land and Estates plc v Brown* 2000 SC 320 (digested at (38) above).

RECTIFICATION AND REDUCTION

(71) Delikes Ltd v Scottish & Newcastle plc
2000 SCLR 163 (Sh Ct) aff'd 2000 SLT (Sh Ct) 67

A company granted a standard security to Scottish & Newcastle over the Carousel Bar, Bellshill. Subsequently, William Fachie, a director and shareholder, arranged to borrow £60,000 from Scottish & Newcastle to convert a bar in the Gatsby Hotel in Wishaw into an Irish bar. The loan was granted on the basis that it too would be secured on the Carousel Bar. The company agreed with Mr Fachie to vary the standard security to include the new loan. A bilateral variation was duly drawn up and executed, but instead of being confined to a loan of £60,000 it extended to all the borrowings of Mr Fachie from Scottish & Newcastle. Later the company sought to have the variation rectified to the effect of restricting the security to £60,000. **Held**: action dismissed. (i) A document could not be rectified under s 8(1)(a) of the Law Reform (Miscellaneous Provisions) (Scotland) Act 1985 where, as here, the parties to that document were different from the parties to the antecedent agreement which the document purported to implement. (ii) But in any event, the pleadings did not disclose a common intention that the security should be restricted to £60,000.

On (i) see **Commentary** p 120. A point to note is that it was accepted on both sides, and by the sheriff principal (at p 70K–L), that s 8 of the Law Reform (Miscellaneous Provisions) (Scotland) Act 1985 does not require that the party seeking rectification be a party to the document. Thus, it would be perfectly competent for the current owner of property to seek rectification of an earlier disposition in the prescriptive progress; but, following the decision in *Delikes*, he would have to do so on the basis of an antecedent agreement between the two parties to that deed.

(72) Norwich Union Life Insurance Society v Tanap Investments VK Ltd (No 2)
2000 SC 515, 2000 SLT 819, 2000 SCLR 1034 (IH)

Norwich Union gave three separate loans, marked by three separate minutes of agreement. In exchange they took a standard security (over Douglas House, Waterloo Street, Glasgow) which referred only to the first minute of agreement. In a case reported at 1997 GWD 32–1634 it was held that the second and third loans were not variations or extensions of the first and so were not covered by the standard security. Norwich Union then applied for rectification of the second and third minutes of agreement to the effect of making them such variations or extensions (and so covered by the standard security). The basic argument was that the parties had the common intention that all three minutes should be covered by the security. Hence, rectification was required to give effect to that common intention. In 1998 the Lord Ordinary allowed proof before answer: see 1999 SLT 204, 1998 SCLR 627. The second defenders appealed. **Held**: that the pleadings disclosed a sufficient case of prior common intention to justify a proof.

A further issue was the title of the second defenders to oppose rectification. They were neither the debtors (who were the first defenders, now in liquidation), nor did they claim to be a third party who had acted in reliance on the unrectified deed, in terms of s 9 of the Law Reform (Miscellaneous Provisions) (Scotland) Act 1985. Rather they seem to have been postponed creditors, whose security would be affected if rectification were granted. The argument of the Norwich Union was that the position of third parties is wholly regulated by s 9. A third party can oppose rectification if and only if a case can be made under that provision. Otherwise, rectification is a question only between the original parties. This argument was rejected by the court. At common law the second defenders would have had title to defend, on the basis that their position would be adversely affected by rectification. Section 9 could not be read as removing that common law right. See **Commentary** p 120.

(73) Baird v Drumpellier & Mount Vernon Estates Ltd (No 2) 2000 GWD 12–427 (OH)

When title to land turned out to be defective, the buyer claimed in warrandice. At an earlier stage in the litigation (see 2000 SC 103 and *Conveyancing 1999* Case (24)) the sellers counterclaimed for rectification of the disposition, by deleting the absolute warrandice and replacing it by simple warrandice. They failed, partly because, though the clause about good and marketable title had been deleted from missives, there was still implied in that contract a term to similar effect. In the current phase of litigation the sellers sought to meet this point by seeking rectification of the missives themselves. **Held**: that no relevant case had been made.

This is yet another example of how difficult it is to rectify missives. Rectification is allowed under s 8(1)(a) of the Law Reform (Miscellaneous Provisions) (Scotland) Act 1985 only if it can be demonstrated that the document failed to express accurately the common intention of the parties to the agreement. But usually there is no prior agreement distinct from the missives themselves, and thus no evidence that the missives departed from what was previously agreed.

One argument used in the case was that there could be a 'common intention of the parties' if both parties held the same view (in this case, of the legal effect of certain words), even though neither had communicated that view to the other. Lord Hamilton reserved his opinion on this point.

The case also illustrates the danger of inserting absolute warrandice as a matter of style. One often sees it in donations, or in sales where the buyer has agreed to 'take title as it stands'. In neither case is it appropriate. The words 'I grant warrandice' mean absolute warrandice: if a lesser warrandice is intended that must be spelled out.

(74) Bank of Ireland v Bass Brewers Ltd
2000 GWD 20–786 and 28–1077 (OH)

This was an application under s 8(1)(b) of the Law Reform (Miscellaneous Provisions) (Scotland) Act 1985 for rectification of a letter of consent by Bass, holders of a floating charge, to the grant of a standard security to the Bank of Ireland. **Held**: proof allowed, notwithstanding that the alleged error on the part of the granter was, not an error in the words used, but an error as to the legal effect of those words. See **Commentary** p 118. Subsequently, rectification was awarded of consent and without proof.

[Another aspect of this decision is digested at (56).]

DILIGENCE AND INSOLVENCY

(75) Halifax plc v Gorman's Trustee 2000 SLT 1409 (OH)

An undischarged bankrupt purchased heritable property and granted a standard security over it. **Held**: that the security was effective. See **Commentary** p 99.

(76) Roy's Trustee, Noter
2000 SLT (Sh Ct) 77 and 2000 SCLR 1105 (sub nom *Wright, Noter*)

A trustee in sequestration, wishing to preserve rights in certain heritable property, sought permission to effect a late registration of a renewal notice under s 14 of the Bankruptcy (Scotland) Act 1985. See **Commentary** p 102. Wright acted as trustee in respect of the sequestration of two different people (Roy and Mackenzie), and identical opinions were issued by the sheriff in each case.

(77) Tewnion's Trustee, Noter 2000 SLT (Sh Ct) 37

The same issue as in the previous case, and decided the same way. See **Commentary** p 102.

(78) Commissioners of Customs and Excise v Zaoui
2000 SLT (Sh Ct) 197 *rev* 2001 SLT 201 (IH)

This and the next case are only marginally conveyancing cases but nevertheless deserve notice. Section 12(3A) of the Bankruptcy (Scotland) Act 1985 (as amended) provides that a petition for sequestration can be dismissed if:

> the debtor forthwith pays or satisfies, or produces written evidence of the payment or satisfaction of, or gives or shows that there is sufficient security for the payment of (i) the debt in respect of which he became apparently insolvent; and (ii) any other debt due by him to the petitioner and any creditor concurring in the petition.

The defender met a petition for his sequestration by offering postponed standard securities. The sheriff allowed this defence and the sheriff principal, in an interesting opinion, declined to disturb the decision. On further appeal to the Inner House the decision was reversed and the sheriff was ordered to award sequestration. The case turned mainly on the word 'forthwith' in s 12(3A). Lord Prosser stated (at p 206B) that 'The sufficiency of any newly given security, like the sufficiency of any pre-existing security, must in my opinion be shown "forthwith".' Moreover the security must not only be shown 'forthwith' to be sufficient but it must be 'given' forthwith.

This decision, in conjunction with the next, may make it difficult for debtors in future to resist sequestration on this ground.

(79) Clydesdale Bank plc v Grantly Developments
2000 SLT 1369, 2000 SCLR 771 (OH)

This case concerned the same issue as the previous one. Richard William Crocket and Graham Duffy were the partners of Grantly Developments, which firm owed £778,065.07 to the Clydesdale Bank. The bank had a security over one property. When it petitioned for the firm's sequestration the defenders offered standard securities over other property. The pursuers doubted whether the security offered would be sufficient. The defence was unsuccessful. Lord Nimmo Smith remarked that 'a standard security is only sufficient security if it is capable of realisation forthwith and will accordingly result in payment of the whole debt without undue delay'.

A related, and earlier, litigation is *Grantly Developments* v *Clydesdale Bank plc* 2000 GWD 6–213 (digested as Case (57) above).

(80) Burns' Tr v Burns 2000 GWD 22–860 (OH)

This case attracted some media publicity. In 1993 William Burns was sequestrated for non-payment of £993 of community charge ('poll tax'). In addition to the campaign he had run in that connection, Burns ran a campaign in relation to his sequestration. According to the Lord Ordinary (Philip):

> The ... administration of the estate has been hindered by the first defender's [ie Burns's] deliberate failure to co-operate with the trustee in any way. To make matters worse, the trustee and other officials concerned with the administration of the estate (including myself) have received hundreds of letters from the first defender couched in abusive, offensive and defamatory terms indicating his refusal to co-operate. The result of the first defender's conduct has been that the expenses of the administration of the estate now amount to about £30,000.

Burns co-owned his house at 18 Shore Road, South Queensferry, with his wife. The trustee wished this to be sold: the free proceeds attributable to the debtor's share was expected to be about £20,000. Section 40 of the Bankruptcy (Scotland) Act 1985 confers an element of discretion on the court where property belonging to a bankrupt is a family home. **Held**: that the house should be sold, but with a grace period of six months.

(81) Nottay's Tr v Nottay 2000 GWD 28–1091 (OH)

Spouses were co-owners of property. The husband disponed his share to his wife 'for love favour and affection'. The following year he was sequestrated, and the trustee in sequestration challenged the transfer as a gratuitous alienation. The wife pled that the narrative clause was untrue. See **Commentary** p 103.

(82) Bank of Scotland v Reid 2000 GWD 22–858 (OH)

Alexander Reid assigned a lease to his daughter Jill. The narrative clause said that the deed was gratuitous. Later an action was raised to reduce the assignation as a gratuitous alienation. The defence was that the narrative clause was inaccurate. See **Commentary** p 104.

RESIDENTIAL CARE FOR THE ELDERLY

(83) Yule v South Lanarkshire Council 2000 SLT 1249, 2001 SCLR 26 (IH)

An elderly lady disponed her house to herself in liferent and to her granddaughter in fee. When, not long afterwards, she had to go into residential care, the local authority took the view that she had voluntarily deprived herself of assets so as to gain entitlement to publicly-funded care. The case affirms the decisions of the Lord Ordinary reported at 1998 SLT 490 and at 1999 SCLR 985 upholding the local authority's determination. See **Commentary** p 121.

(84) Robertson v Fife Council 2000 SLT 1226 (OH)

A decision substantially similar to the previous one. See **Commentary** p 122.

COMMON GOOD

(85) Stirling Council, Petrs 2000 GWD 18–722 (OH)

Permission was granted for the sale of a museum hall in Bridge of Allan, part of the common good, on the basis that it was in poor condition and could not reasonably be restored. However, the permission was subject to a number of conditions, including that (i) the purchasers must be taken bound to retain and restore the front elevation and (ii) the proceeds should be held as a common good fund for the benefit of the local community.

For the background to cases such as this, see Andrew Ferguson, 'Common Good Land' 2000 SLT (News) 7.

PART II

STATUTORY DEVELOPMENTS

(A) ABOLITION OF FEUDAL TENURE ETC (SCOTLAND) ACT 2000 (asp 5)

This long and complex Act abolishes the feudal system of land tenure, and makes important transitional provisions for the preservation of feudal real burdens and for compensation for loss of feuduty. Other provisions abolish thirlage, the conveyancing privileges of barony titles, and tailzies (entails). The length of new leases is restricted to 175 years. It is provided, retrospectively, that a description in a standard security is sufficient if it identifies the subjects. The last two provisions came into force on royal assent, on 9 June 2000, but otherwise the Act is mainly not yet in force. See **Commentary** p 123.

(B) ADULTS WITH INCAPACITY (SCOTLAND) ACT 2000 (asp 4)

This is a comprehensive reform of the law. Most of it is irrelevant to conveyancing, but it changes the rules about continuing powers of attorney. To be effective these will have to meet certain requirements and also be registered with a new official called the Public Guardian. In addition, our old friend the curator bonis goes to his long home, and some of the new rules have property law impact. For example, s 56 provides that an 'intervention order' which affects heritable property must be entered on the title sheet of the property in question, and the same is true of guardianship orders under s 61. Whether this system will be workable remains to be seen.

(C) NATIONAL PARKS (SCOTLAND) ACT 2000 (asp 10)

This Act provides for the creation of 'national parks'. Each such park will have its own 'authority' with a variety of powers.

(D) FINANCE ACT 2000

Increased stamp duty for conveyances on sale

Section 114 increases, yet again, the rates of stamp duty for conveyances on sale. (For last year's increase, see *Conveyancing 1999* p 31.) The new rates are:

Consideration	Duty	
0–£60,0000	nil	(unchanged)
£60,001–£250,000	1%	(unchanged)
£250,001–£500,000	3%	(up from 2.5%)
£500,001–	4%	(up from 3.5%)

These rates apply to all deeds executed on or after 28 March 2000 except where executed in pursuance of a contract made on or before 21 March 2000.

Stamp duty—other developments

Section 115 amends the duty chargeable on leases of less than one year of furnished dwelling houses. The duty will now be £5 where the rent does not exceed £5,000 (formerly £500).

Similarly, for leases of other premises of seven years or less, the duty will be nil if the average annual rent does not exceed £5,000 (formerly £500); and 1% if the rent exceeds this amount.

Both of these changes affect instruments executed on or after 28 March 2000.

Section 116 corrects an error made in the Finance Act 1999, so that stamp duty becomes chargeable on leases of *exactly* seven years. This is retrospective, so that leases executed between 30 September 1999 and 27 March 2000 which were correctly stamped in accordance with the applicable law are deemed to be insufficiently stamped with effect from 28 March 2000.

Section 117 and Sched 33 introduce a new power to make regulations for (*inter alia*) altering the categories of document liable to stamp duty. This is, or at least is said to be, an anti-avoidance power, and may become particularly important as the rising rates of stamp duty make avoidance increasingly attractive.

Sections 118 and 119 also strike in the realm of alleged avoidance, although they catch transactions which until recently would have been thought to be entirely innocent. Section 118 is aimed at transactions in which land is transferred in return for other property, for instance exempt gilt-edged securities. (Exchanges of land for other land are already caught by s 241 of the Finance Act 1994, although such exchanges can still be structured as sales, to avoid *both* instruments being liable to duty.) The duty will generally be charged on a maximum of the market value of the land transferred, although it may be less than this if the property transferred is worth less than the land received in exchange.

Section 119 of the Finance Act 2000 (which takes precedence over s 118 where both could apply) treats as a transfer on sale the transfer of land to a company with which the transferor is connected. This applies to gifts of the land, or situations where securities (whether in the transferee company or otherwise) are transferred in return for the land. This provision in particular may restrict the ability of those trading as sole traders or partnerships to incorporate without the possibility of a large stamp duty charge.

Section 120 provides a complex range of exceptions from the preceding two sections—for example, transfers from nominees or trustees (at least where there is no avoidance involved); and s 121 applies the same rules to leases with connected companies as apply to transfers of land outright.

Section 123 deals with the definition of associated companies for group relief from stamp duty. It is made somewhat more restricted, in line with the rules which apply to grouping for other tax purposes. This applies to transfers between companies and, by s 125, to leases as well.

Section 128 tightens up the rules on renunciations of leases. Any document evidencing the renunciation is now to be treated as a deed effecting the renunciation. This is apparently directed against arrangements whereby renunciations take effect by operation of law rather than by written agreement.

Section 130 introduces an exemption for transfers to 'qualifying landlords', such as housing associations.

Further details are awaited of changes to cope with electronic conveyancing; and of a proposed exemption from stamp duty on property transactions 'within Britain's most disadvantaged communities to stimulate the property market and encourage urban renewal' (to quote HM Treasury).

Landfill tax

The promised 'escalator' of landfill tax rates starts to rise, with an increase from £10 to £11 per tonne (s 140).

(E) EXTENSION OF LAND REGISTER

The Land Registration (Scotland) Act 1979 (Commencement No 14) Order 2000 extends the Land Register to the County of Midlothian as from 1 April 2001. Currently around 40% of all properties are registered on the Land Register.

(F) APPLICATION FORMS UNDER THE RIGHT-TO-BUY LEGISLATION

A new form has been prescribed by the Right to Purchase (Application Form) (Scotland) Order 2000, SI 2000/120, made under s 63(1) of the Housing (Scotland) Act 1987.

PART III

OTHER MATERIAL

(A) MORTGAGE RIGHTS (SCOTLAND) BILL

This is a Bill to provide discretionary controls over the enforcement of residential 'mortgages'. See **Commentary** p 91.

(B) HOUSING (SCOTLAND) BILL

The Housing (Scotland) Bill, introduced to the Scottish Parliament on 18 December 2000, is a substantial measure, running to 101 sections and nine schedules. Among the subjects covered are: homelessness; the introduction of a new 'Scottish secure tenancy' for tenants of councils and other social landlords; the tightening up of the right-to-buy rules in respect of new tenancies (by amending Part III of the Housing (Scotland) Act 1987), with smaller discounts and longer qualifying periods; the introduction of a new and uniform regulatory framework for social landlords; the conversion of Scottish Homes into an executive agency; and new provisions about improvement grants.

(C) REAL BURDENS/TITLE CONDITIONS (SCOTLAND) BILL

The final *Report on Real Burdens* (Scot Law Com No 181) by the Scottish Law Commission was published in October 2000. It includes a draft Title Conditions (Scotland) Bill, which is expected to form the basis of legislation to be introduced to the Scottish Parliament during 2001. See **Commentary** p 75. The text is available at www.scotlawcom.gov.uk

(D) PARTNERSHIP

Far-reaching reforms of the law of partnership are suggested in a consultation paper on *Partnership Law* issued jointly by the Law Commission and the Scottish Law Commission (SLC DP No 111) on 13 September 2000. Some of these impact on the conveyancer—for example, proposals for continuity of partnership notwithstanding changes in the partners. There is a commentary on the paper, by David Guild, at 2000 SLT (News) 315. The text is available at www.scotlawcom.gov.uk

(E) NUISANCE HEDGES

The Scottish Executive issued a paper seeking views on the nuisance caused by fast-growing hedges such as leyland cypress (*cupressocyparis leylandii*). The text is available at www.scotland.gov.uk/consultations/leylandii-00.htm

(F) CARBETH (AND OTHER) HUTTERS

The Scottish Executive issued a paper on 15 December 2000 seeking views on whether statutory protection should be introduced for Carbeth (and other) hutters. A 'hutter' is a person who has the use of a hut which has been built or acquired primarily for use as a holiday or weekend home. The land itself is leased, usually from year to year and at a low rent. Research suggests that there are around 600 huts in Scotland on some 27 sites. The largest and most prominent site is at Carbeth, near Blanefield in Stirlingshire, which has around 170 huts. Most huts date from the 1930s and are used by people who are middle-aged to elderly. If legislation were to be introduced, it would comprise both security of tenure and rent control. Inevitably it would be quite complex.

(G) SHARP v THOMSON

On 24 October 2000 the Minister for Justice gave the following Parliamentary answer: 'The Executive is aware that the case of *Sharp* v *Thomson* raised a number of issues in relation to the purchase of heritage from registered companies. To ensure that the implications of this case are fully considered and the wider context of current reviews on the law of diligence and land attachment is taken into account, I have invited the Scottish Law Commission to examine the position, and they have accepted the following reference: To consider the implications of the decision of the House of Lords in *Sharp* v *Thomson* 1997 SC (HL) 66 and to make recommendations as to possible reform of the law.' A discussion paper is expected to be issued for consultation during 2001. See **Commentary** p 93.

(H) FORESHORE AND SEABED

On 28 January 2000 the Minister for Justice announced that he had sent the Scottish Law Commission the following reference: 'Taking account of the Land Reform Action Plan, to consider the existing law of the foreshore and seabed, and to advise on possible reforms, with a view to improving clarity and consistency.' A discussion paper is expected to be issued for consultation during 2001.

(I) SCOTTISH CONVEYANCING AND EXECUTRY SERVICES BOARD

The Board's annual report for 1999/2000 discloses that there were four successful applications for registration as a licensed conveyancer or executry practitioner. This brings the total to nine. Two offer services directly to the public. The Board continues to be concerned about the small number of applications. The annual cost of the Board is around £150,000. The Board now has a website: www.scesb.co.uk

(J) RESEARCH INTO EXPERIENCES OF HOUSE BUYERS

Recent research by the Scottish Consumer Council on the experiences of house buyers is summarised in *Home Truths: A Report on Research into the Experiences of Recent House Buyers in Scotland* (2000; ISBN 0 907067 85 9). In general, satisfaction rates were relatively high, at around 70% (compared with 45% in a recent survey in England and Wales).

There is some useful discussion of the issue of multiple surveys. The scale of the problem was found to be quite small. 53% of those questioned were successful with their first offer, and most of the rest with their second. The idea of a survey provided by the seller was opposed by 58%, mainly because of doubts about reliability. The SCC suggest instead an independent survey prepared for buyers, with the costs shared, or met by the successful buyer (pp 66–67). This would be a market-led, voluntary scheme.

The research suggests a lack of information from solicitors to clients on certain subjects. Only 54% of those questioned said that they had been given information on the burdens affecting their property; and in the case of tenements only 55% said that the arrangements for common repairs had been explained to them. Broadly similar findings are contained in a survey carried out for the Scottish Law Commission, and reproduced at the end of the Commission's *Report on Real Burdens* (Scot Law Com No 181, 2000).

(K) MORTGAGE REGULATION

The (UK) Government announced that the residential mortgage business is to be regulated in future by the new Financial Services Authority. The FSA has issued a consultation paper, available from them at 25 North Colonnade, Canary Wharf, London E14 5HS, or at www.fas.gov.uk/pubs/cp70/ At present it seems unlikely that there will be a regulatory impact on solicitors.

(L) CML HANDBOOK

The Council of Mortgage Lenders (CML) published *The CML Lenders Handbook for Scotland*. See **Commentary** p 83.

(M) NEW BOOKS

Sir Crispin Agnew of Lochnaw, *Crofting Law* (T&T Clark, 2000; ISBN 0 567 00547 X)

Council of Mortgage Lenders, *The CML Lenders Handbook for Scotland* (CML, 2000, ISBN 1 872423 50 7)

Ian Davis and Alistair Rennie (eds), *Registration of Title Practice Book* (2nd edn, 2000; ISBN 0953 418 014)

Ann Faulds and June Hyslop, *Scottish Roads Law* (Butterworths, 2000; ISBN 0 406 081 743)

Roderick R M Paisley, *Land Law* (W Green/Sweet & Maxwell, 2000; ISBN 0414 013 832)

Roderick R M Paisley and Douglas J Cusine (eds), *Unreported Property Cases from the Sheriff Courts* (W Green/Sweet & Maxwell, 2000; ISBN 0 414 013387)

C Parkes and J Thornley, *Deer: Law and Liabilities* (Swan Hill: Shrewsbury, 2000; ISBN 1 84037 096 3)

Kenneth Reid and George Gretton, *Conveyancing 1999* (T&T Clark, 2000; ISBN 0 567 00564 X)

Kenneth Reid and Reinhard Zimmermann (eds), *A History of Private Law in Scotland*: vol 1 Introduction and Property; vol 2 Obligations (Oxford University Press, 2000; ISBN 0 19 829941 9)

Jeremy Rowan-Robinson and Donna McKenzie Skene (eds), *Countryside Law in Scotland* (T&T Clark, 2000; ISBN 0 567 00538 0)

(N) NEW ARTICLES

A D Anderson, 'Community Rights to Buy and Rights of Public Responsible Access' (2000) 68 *Scottish Law Gazette* 42

A D Anderson, 'Superiorities—The Beginning of the End' (2000) 68 *Scottish Law Gazette* 132

Hazel Bett, 'Transfer of Title in Matrimonial Disputes' (2000) 48 *Greens Property Law Bulletin* 1

David A Brand, 'Time for Special Destinations to Die?' 2000 SLT (News) 203

David A Brand, 'New Life for Notaries? The Challenge of E-Commerce' 2000 *Juridical Review* 141

David A Brand, 'Parts and Pertinents in Conveyancing—What Exactly does this Mean?' (2000) 5 *Scottish Law & Practice Quarterly* 386

STEWART BRYMER, 'Reference to Independent Determination' (2000) 43 *Greens Property Law Bulletin* 2

STEWART BRYMER, 'Length of Leases' (2000) 44 *Greens Property Law Bulletin* 3

STEWART BRYMER, '*Sharp* v *Thomson*—an Update' (2000) 45 *Greens Property Law Bulletin* 1

STEWART BRYMER, 'Service Charges' (2000) 46 *Greens Property Law Bulletin* 2

STEWART BRYMER, 'Rent Review: A New Dawn? Nature and Purpose of Rent Review' (2000) 47 *Greens Property Law Bulletin* 3

COLIN C CAMPBELL, 'The Ownership of Corporeal Property as a Separate Tenement' 2000 *Juridical Review* 39

COLIN C CAMPBELL, 'Charred or Chosen? Clauses dealing with Risk and Insurance in Contracts for the Sale of Heritable Property' (2000) 5 *Scottish Law & Practice Quarterly* 250

DOUGLAS CUSINE, 'Local Authorities, Superiors' Consents and Planning Permission' (2000) 5 *Scottish Law & Practice Quarterly* 315

DOUGLAS CUSINE, 'Real Burdens in the New Millennium' (2000) 43 *Greens Property Law Bulletin* 1

ANDREW FERGUSON, 'Common Good Land' 2000 SLT (News) 7

HUGH HENDERSON, 'The Stamping of Dispositions of Licensed Premises' (2000) 46 *Greens Property Law Bulletin* 1

G J JUNOR, 'Bearing Witness to the Deed: The Requirements of Writing (Scotland) Act 1995 section 3 etc' (2000) 68 *Scottish Law Gazette* 8

G J JUNOR, 'Sale of Security Subjects: Applying the Free Proceeds' (2000) 5 *Scottish Law & Practice Quarterly* 72

WILLIAM NEILSON, 'Residential Care Fees: Protecting the Assets' 2000 SLT (News) 330

ADELE J NICOL and SARAH M DEWAR, 'The Abolition of Feudal Tenure etc (Scotland) Act 2000' (2000) 47 *Greens Property Law Bulletin* 1 and (2000) 48 *Greens Property Law Bulletin* 3

RODERICK R M PAISLEY, 'Property Law Update' (2000) 5 *Scottish Law & Practice Quarterly* 76, 174 and 432

RODERICK R M PAISLEY and CORNELIUS G VAN DER MERWE, 'Perpetual Roads: A Never-Ending Story?' (2000) 5 *Scottish Law & Practice Quarterly* 196 and 333

REGISTERS OF SCOTLAND, 'Land Registration Questions' (2000) 46 *Greens Property Law Bulletin* 5 (but this should be read subject to the clarifications at (2000) 48 *Greens Property Law Bulletin* 6)

Donald A Reid, 'The Landfill Tax Credit Scheme' (2000) 46 *Greens Property Law Bulletin* 4

Kenneth Reid, 'The Title Conditions Bill' 45 *Journal of the Law Society of Scotland* (November 2000, 25)

Robert Rennie, 'The Modern Missive' 2000 SLT (News) 65

Robert Rennie, 'Conclusion of Missives in the Modern Age' (2000) 5 *Scottish Law & Practice Quarterly* 346

Robert Rennie, 'To *Sharp* v *Thomson*—an Heir' 2000 SLT (News) 247

Kenneth Ross, 'Contaminated Land' 45 *Journal of the Law Society of Scotland* (August 2000, 36)

Liz Scobie and Anne Fergusson, 'Property Aspects of PFI Transactions' (2000) 44 *Greens Property Law Bulletin* 1

Alastair Smith, 'Keep on Keeping Open: *Highland and Universal Properties Ltd* v *Safeway Properties Ltd*' (2000) 4 *Edinburgh Law Review* 336

P F Smith, 'Owning Flats: Scottish or English Style?' (2000) 5 *Scottish Law & Practice Quarterly* 36

Andrew J M Steven, 'Keeping the Goalposts in Sight' 2000 SLT (News) 143

Debra Storr, 'Aberdeen Solicitors' Property Centre—A Case Study' (2000) 68 *Scottish Law Gazette* 44

Scott Crichton Styles, '*Sharp* Pains for Scots Property Law: the Case of *Burnett's Tr* v *Grainger*' 2000 SLT (News) 305

PART IV

COMMENTARY

SERVITUDES AND RIGHTS OF WAY

Why can the public use roads?

Often property inquiry certificates contain the reassuring intelligence that the road *ex adverso* the subjects has been taken over for maintenance. And this confirmation that the road is 'public' is likely to satisfy most purchasers. For it means not only that the road will be maintained at public expense but also— or so it is generally assumed—that the road is one which the public at large can use. This removes the need to worry further about access. But is the inference a safe one? Are all 'public' roads public rights of way? In particular, what of those which are too new for prescriptive possession to have established the rights of the public? Is the public entitled to use such a road and, if so, why?

Some consideration was given to this question in *MacKinnon* v *Argyll and Bute Council*.[1] A Council adopted a way as a public road under s 16 of the Roads (Scotland) Act 1984. The adoption was opposed by the pursuer, who variously owned and leased the land which included the way. One of his arguments was that the way was not a 'road' within the meaning of s 16. Section 16[2] empowers a roads authority to add a road to the list of public roads. 'Road' is defined in s 151(1) of the Roads (Scotland) Act 1984 to mean any way 'over which there is a public right of passage'. It followed from this definition that a public right of passage must already be in existence before a road can be adopted. In the present case, it was argued, there had been no such public right of passage.

This construction of the statute seems correct. So the question was whether there had existed a public right of passage prior to the road being adopted; and that in turn led to a consideration of the meaning of 'public right of passage'.

It was accepted that a public right of way in the strict sense must always qualify as a public right of passage. But on the basis of some previous cases, mainly concerned with the importation of the Roads (Scotland) Act 1984 definition into criminal statutes,[3] Lord Osborne concluded that less would do:[4]

---

1 2000 GWD 11–371. Other aspects of this case are explored by R R M Paisley at (2000) 4 *Scottish Law & Practice Quarterly* 432–434.
2 And also s 1 of the 1984 Act, imposing a statutory duty to maintain a list of public roads.
3 In particular *Cowie* v *Strathclyde Regional Council* First Division, 8 July 1986 (unreported); *Beattie* v *Scott* 1990 SCCR 435; and *Dick* v *Walkingshaw* 1995 SLT 1264.
4 Page 26 of the transcript.

> In my view, 'a public right of passage' may properly be described as a permission, express or implied, derived from those having legal right to control the use of the way concerned, for public use of that way; or established acquiescence or tolerance by those persons having such public use.

Prescriptive possession was not required. Indeed the relevant provision in the Prescription Act[1] was confined to public rights of way in the strict sense.

At first sight this seems good news for those wishing to make use of roads. A road or other way can be used, on this view, even in the absence of a public right of way. The difficulty, however, is that what is freely given, by consent or acquiescence, may also be freely withdrawn. Lord Osborne went on to say that:

> A 'public right of passage', so defined, may be terminated by those having such legal right [ie the right to control the use of the way], unless it has come to be associated with a public right of way, as normally understood, or with some statutory public right, which would prevent termination.

This analysis gives rise to a problem. Take the following example. A Council adopts a road. At the time of adoption there is no public right of way, only a public right of passage attributable to the owner's acquiescence. What is the position after adoption? Can the owner terminate the public rights, in the manner indicated by Lord Osborne, or does the very act of adoption—the change of status from private road to public road—confer an irrevocable public right? This last suggestion is firmly rejected in a new book on roads law, *Scottish Roads Law* by Ann Faulds and June Hyslop:[2]

> There is no relationship between a public right of passage and the public status of a road. The public status of a road relates only to responsibility for maintenance. It does not create or sustain a public right of passage over the road.

Certainly there is nothing in the Roads (Scotland) Act 1984 which suggests the contrary. But this approach leads to the unpalatable conclusion that there may be 'public' roads over which the public has no rights.

Even if that is correct—and perhaps only further litigation will make the position clear—there are factors which, taken together, may go far to eliminate the problem. First, there will often be a public right of way—and almost always if the road is more than 20 years' old. Second, many roads are adopted at the request of a developer or other owner; and since public rights of way can be created by express grant,[3] there is a powerful argument that the very act of seeking adoption constitutes the creation of a public right of way. *MacKinnon* was highly unusual in that adoption was opposed by the owner. Third, even in the absence of a public right of way, there may be a common law right of 'highway'—although the incidence and scope of this venerable right are unclear.[4] Finally, at least in cases where the road is owned by the roads authority, and

---

1 Prescription and Limitation (Scotland) Act 1973, s 3(3).
2 Page 41.
3 D J Cusine and R R M Paisley, *Servitudes and Rights of Way* (1998) para 19–11.
4 See further D J Cusine and R R M Paisley, *Servitudes and Rights of Way* paras 18–03 to 18–10.

perhaps in some other cases too, the road may be treated as having been irrevocably dedicated to public use. That proposition seems to have been the unarticulated[1] premise of the case discussed next.

Public roads and ransom strips

Consider the following. A Council acquires land, whether voluntarily or by compulsory purchase. It constructs a road. Not all of the land is metalled, for there is a strip of rough ground on either side. Since the road is a public road, owned by the Council, the public has a right to use it, on principles just discussed. But does that right extend to the unmetalled strips? What, in other words, is the road over which the public has rights?

This issue arose sharply in *Elmford Ltd* v *City of Glasgow Council (No 2)*.[2] Strathclyde Regional Council acquired land by compulsory purchase under powers contained in the Roads (Scotland) Act 1984. A road was duly built. Developers, who owned adjacent land, wished to build a service station. In order for the service station to be usable it was necessary to take access over an unmetalled strip. Glasgow Council, the successors of Strathclyde, refused to allow access, at least without payment. Their refusal was challenged.

On the facts, it was held that the strip was not part of the road. This was partly because the fairly detailed description of the road made for the purposes of listing did not include the strip, and partly because photographic evidence showed an overgrown area which seemed not intended for public passage.[3] In other roads, of course, the position might be different. 'Road', after all, is defined in the Roads (Scotland) Act 1984 as including the verge.[4] Clearly the position will depend on the facts on the ground.

More important is the general principle. According to Lord Clarke:[5]

> In my judgment the acquisition by an authority of land . . . in connection with the construction of a road is not to be taken, by itself, as the equivalent of a dedication of that land, in its entirety, to public passage.

An authority might well acquire more land than it needs for the road itself. Extra land might be needed for the initial construction, for possible future road-widening—or, it is tempting to add, to create a ransom strip.

The argument is plausible, though we understand that the decision has been appealed. Whether the decision is correct in policy is a matter of taste. To some

---

1 *Elmford Ltd* v *City of Glasgow Council (No 2)* 2001 SC 267. Or at least barely articulated. But note the following passage (p 273 D–G): 'Senior Counsel for the petitioners submitted that once something is a road there is a public right of passage over it. As he put it, it is the existence of a road that creates the public right of way . . . The road, before it was listed, already existed as road—listing of it simply imposed an obligation of maintenance upon the roads authority in respect of it.'
2 2001 SC 267.
3 This is the legal principle of the hidden verge (*vergens ad myopiam*).
4 Roads (Scotland) Act 1984, s 151(1).
5 At p 278D.

it may seem wrong that a Council should be able to acquire land with public money for a public road, and yet deny the public use of some of that land. To others there may be no reason why a Council should contribute to the profits of a private developer.[1]

Access to landlocked property

The developers in *Elmford Ltd* v *City of Glasgow Council* were not landlocked, but could obtain access to the public road in a different way. The question of whether land which is landlocked is entitled to special privileges has been controversial. The institutional writers tended to take the view that the owner of landlocked land had a right of access, subject to qualifications; but up until now there was no decided case directly in point, and modern *obiter dicta* are rather conflicting.[2]

The issue arose, however, in the important case of *Bowers* v *Kennedy*.[3] The facts were somewhat unusual. In 1945 land was divided into two plots (A and B). The plots were sold at much the same time, but A was sold first. Since plot B was landlocked, a servitude of access in its favour was reserved in the disposition of plot A. Years passed, and plot B ceased to be actively used. Both plots changed hands. A dispute then arose as to whether the servitude of access had been lost by negative prescription. It was held by the First Division that, if 20 years of non-use could be proved, the servitude would indeed be extinguished. But that was not the end of the matter. Even in the absence of an express servitude, there would have been an implied right to use the access. Though such an implied right has often been characterised as an implied servitude, in substance it is a right of access inherent in the idea of ownership itself.[4] That was the analysis found in the institutional writers. In other words, the very fact that plot B was landlocked was sufficient to create a right of access over plot A.

At first sight, this new distinction—between (i) a right of access as an implied servitude, and (ii) a right of access arising as an incident of ownership—might seem no more than a matter of analytical preference. In fact it was crucial for determination of the case. An ordinary servitude right prescribes after 20 years' non-use. A right arising as an incident of ownership, according to the court, does not:[5]

---

1 The Council's argument on this point was (p 277G): 'There was no duty on the respondents to enhance the profitability of the petitioners by affording them, gratuitously, access over land which was not a road. There was no obligation on the respondents to dispose of land or land rights gratuitously to encourage development.'

2 For a complete review, see D J Cusine and R R M Paisley, *Servitudes and Rights of Way* pp 363–377.

3 2000 SC 555, 2000 SLT 1006.

4 2000 SLT 1006 at 1010L–1011A *per* Lord President Rodger: 'The fact of the matter is that the doctrine of implied grant or reservation of servitudes, so far as applied to ways of necessity, is a means—fiction, if you will—by which the law rationalises the operation of the rule that the owner of an enclave has a right to the necessary access for the enjoyment of his property. In other words, in such cases "servitudes" of this kind are in substance a manifestation of the right of access which the owner of land must have, if he is to enjoy the possession of his land, and which the law accordingly implies.'

5 2000 SLT 1006 at 1010H *per* Lord President Rodger.

The right to free ish and entry, and the resulting right of access are 'necessary concomitants of property' and therefore, like the right of property itself, they do not prescribe . . . Were it otherwise, and the right of access could prescribe if not exercised for 20 years, this would be tantamount to saying that the owner was obliged to visit his property and use the right of access on pain of losing the right to enjoy his property. Such a conclusion would be inconsistent with the very nature of ownership. The true position is that an owner can choose not to visit his property and exercise his implied right of access, without running any risk of losing his right to enjoy his property. In that sense the exercise of the implied rights of ish and entry and of access may be described as a *res merae facultatis*.[1]

When applied to the facts of the case, the results were these. Assuming non-use could be proved, the express servitude of access was lost after 20 years. But it was then immediately replaced by the right of access inherent in the right of ownership (or it may be that that right was always held concurrently with the express servitude). Accordingly, access could continue to be exercised, albeit on a difference basis.

The novelty of this decision lies in the view that, in cases of landlocked property, there is an inherent right of access which replaces any right which might otherwise have arisen on the doctrine of implied servitudes. The doctrine of implied servitudes remains intact in other cases. It would be potentially applicable, for example, if the access were merely a second access, so that the dominant tenement was not actually landlocked. And it remains intact in cases not involving access. But for landlocked land, the implied servitude is transformed into a right inherent in ownership; or, perhaps more accurately, the inherent right of access is treated as a special type of implied servitude, with special features.[2]

It will require further case law to give a fuller picture of this inherent right of access. On the basis of *Bowers* v *Kennedy* itself it is possible to say the following. First, the right is available over the other property involved in the subdivision. The owner of plot B has a right over plot A. He has no right over other property. Second, if there was a route in use before the subdivision, the access is by that route. Third, the access is of the same *type* as prior to subdivision. Thus, a history of vehicular access would mean that the inherent right was also one of vehicular access. In a sheriff court case, *Mackie* v *Donaldson*,[3] decided at much the same time as *Bowers*, it was suggested that vehicular access would be allowed even without prior use if this had been within the contemplation of the parties at the

---

1 And hence as imprescriptible: see Prescription and Limitation (Scotland) Act 1973, Sched 3(c).

2 That is the view which seems to be taken in the subsequent case of *Inverness Seafield Development Co Ltd* v *D C S Mackintosh* 2001 SLT 118 (discussed below). According to Lord President Rodger (at pp 120L–121A), where land is landlocked, following a subdivision, 'the law would imply a reservation of a servitude of access to the retained land over the option land. But, since any implied right of access or implied reservation of access arises out of necessity, necessity also dictates its duration. It will last as long as necessity requires, but it will also cease or be extinguished when it is no longer necessary . . . [T]he implied right of access itself would cease or, to put the matter another way, the implied servitude of access would be extinguished'.

3 31 May 2000, Hamilton Sheriff Court, noted in R R M Paisley, 'Property Law Update' (2000) 5 *Scottish Law & Practice Quarterly* 432 at 435.

time of the subdivision (*eg* because it was known that the acquirer of the landlocked property intended to build a garage). Fourth, the servient owner is free to substitute a different route provided it is also suitable. Fifth, the inherent right cannot usually be lost. Negative prescription does not apply, as has already been seen; and the court doubted whether the right could be abandoned by the owner in a manner that would bind successors. However, and finally, the right is lost altogether if an alternative means of access becomes available—presumably even a means which is less convenient. Whether it then revives if that means comes to be lost in turn is unclear. Apart from the last two, these characteristics are already familiar from the law of (implied) servitudes.

The change effected by *Bowers* should not be exaggerated. It is a change in doctrinal attribution rather than in the availability of access rights. *Bowers* does not mean that access is now available in cases where it would not have been available before. The rules remain much as previously developed for implied servitudes. In particular, *Bowers* continues to require a subdivision. In other words, in order to claim access—now, as before—it has to be shown that at some time in the past the landlocked property was part of the other property over which access is now claimed. Thus, the decision does not assist in a case where the two properties have always been separately owned. Although access was said to be inherent in ownership, the court was not willing to go so far as to say that that was true in all cases. But nor did the court exclude the possibility. The words are carefully chosen:[1]

> Counsel for the pursuers drew attention to the potentially far reaching implications of the argument that the owner of an enclave has a right to access across the land of his neighbours, even where the lands have not been in single ownership ... It is unnecessary to examine this wider argument in the present case since, if the law does not accord a right to access to an enclave where the lands have been split off from a single estate, it is unlikely that the owner of the enclave can derive such a right on a more general basis.

The issue remains open for another day.

Access implied in missives

An early casualty of *Bowers v Kennedy* was *Inverness Seafield Development Company Ltd v D C S Mackintosh*.[2] This also concerned landlocked land, and, as in *Bowers*, the need for access was anticipated at the time of the subdivision—but not, crucially, at the stage of missives. The defenders were selling one plot (A) and keeping another (B). The retained plot B was landlocked and required access through plot A. Accordingly, the defenders preferred a disposition containing an express reservation of a servitude of access. Their right to do was disputed by the pursuers, on the basis that no provision for such a servitude had been

---

1 2000 SLT 1006 at 1009I–J *per* Lord President Rodger.
2 2001 SLT 118.

made in the missives.[1] The case was heard by the Outer House in 1999.[2] In those pre-*Bowers* days, the law was that, on granting a disposition in circumstances such as these, a servitude of access would be impliedly reserved. Thus, the owners of plot B would receive a servitude. That being the case, Lord Johnston was prepared to hold that a right to a servitude was implied into the missives also. This meant that—the problem having been spotted before the disposition was granted—the sellers could insist on an *express* servitude in the disposition. The improvement in the sellers' position was one of form only. Instead of an implied servitude they would receive an express servitude; but the content of the right in both cases would be identical. The practical advantages of receiving an express servitude were obvious—not least that the servitude would be entered on the Land Register.[3]

The purchasers appealed and the case was heard by the First Division.[4] Shortly before, the same Division had decided, in *Bowers* v *Kennedy*, that the implied access conferred on landlocked property was, at root, attributable to a right inherent in ownership. Crucially, its content was therefore different from that of an ordinary servitude—and in particular it was vulnerable to extinction in the event of an alternative means of access becoming available. It followed, therefore, that to allow the sellers an express *servitude* would be to put them in a different, and probably better, position than under the general law of implied rights. The appeal therefore was allowed, and the purchasers were held entitled to a conveyance without a servitude. This did not mean that the sellers were denied access, of course; but access could be taken only on the basis of the right inherent in ownership.

Reform

The *Report on Real Burdens* by the Scottish Law Commission[5] contains several recommendations on servitudes. Two may be mentioned here.[6]

As the law currently stands, there is a fixed list of servitudes. Only rights which appear on this list can be created as servitudes. In theory, the court has power to add to the list, but in modern times the power has not been exercised. The Scottish Law Commission proposes that the fixed list be abandoned in cases where a servitude is created by writing followed by registration.[7] In the Commission's view, there can be no reason for restricting the types of servitude

---

1 Unusually, their action took the form of an adjudication in implement of missives.
2 1999 GWD 31–1497 (*Conveyancing 1999* Case (19), discussed at pp 48–49).
3 On that basis we welcomed the decision last year: see pp 48–49 of *Conveyancing 1999*. Compare, however, Lord President Rodger (2001 SLT 118 at pp 121–122): 'If the defender's [*ie* owner of plot B] only contention were that, where on conveyance the law imputes a right of access to the defender over the option land, it should equally impute an implied term conferring that right into any preceding missives, then that legal analysis might simply be regarded as somewhat over-refined. In itself it might not be of any real practical significance.'
4 2001 SLT 118.
5 Scot Law Com No 181 (2000) (available on www.scotlawcom.gov.uk).
6 The full recommendations will be found in Part 12 of the Report.
7 *Report on Real Burdens* paras 12.22 to 12.25.

where proper notice has been given by registration. But the fixed list would remain for servitudes created by implication or by prescription. This change would bring Scots law into line with the law in most other countries. It would not mean that all rights could be constituted as servitudes, regardless of content. To qualify, a right would still have to adhere to the general characteristics of a servitude—in particular it would have to be praedial in character, burdening one property for the benefit of another property. Examples of rights which would benefit from the proposal are rights of parking and rights to erect a sign.

The change suggested would of course apply only to new rights. One of the Commission's other recommendations, however, is retrospective in character. There has been a persistent, though probably ill-founded, doubt as to whether the current fixed list of servitudes includes a right to lead pipes or cables. Where the pipes carry water, this is no more than the servitude of aqueduct, familiar from Roman law, and is undoubtedly valid. But the position is less clear where other substances are carried, or are carried by means other than pipes. It has been held in the sheriff court that a right to transmit electricity by overhead cable cannot be constituted as a servitude.[1] The Commission recommends that the doubts be removed, and in relation to existing as well as to new servitudes.[2] The relevant provision in the draft Title Conditions (Scotland) Bill[3] (which is included in the Report) reads:

(1) A right to lead a pipe, cable, wire or other such enclosed unit over or under land for any purpose may be constituted as a positive servitude.

(2) It shall be deemed always to have been competent to constitute a right such as is mentioned in subsection (1) above as a servitude.

A Bill based on the Law Commission's recommendations—the Title Conditions (Scotland) Bill—is expected to be introduced to the Scottish Parliament before the end of 2001.

LEASES

Exclusivity clauses: do they bind successors?

The Gyle Shopping Centre, situated in the western outskirts of Edinburgh, was originally owned by Edinburgh District Council. In 1995 the Council leased Unit 41 to Optical Express for a period of 25 years. By a separate back letter, granted at the same time, the Council agreed that they would not allow any other unit to be primarily used for trading as an optician. This is known as an exclusivity agreement. The lease was registered in the Books of Council and Session: the back letter was not. Despite being a long lease it was not recorded in the Register

1 *Neill* v *Scobbie* 1993 GWD 13–887. For criticism see *eg* D J Cusine and R R M Paisley, *Servitudes and Rights of Way* (1998) para 3–44.
2 *Report on Real Burdens* para 12.26.
3 Section 73.

of Sasines, but that did not prejudice its validity as a real right, for in 1995 Midlothian was still a Sasine area, and in such areas both short and long leases are capable of coming under the protection of the Leases Act 1449.[1]

In 1997 the Centre was sold to Marks & Spencers and Safeways *pro indiviso*. In January 2000 the new landlords decided to lease another unit, Unit 56, to Vision Express, who were opticians. Optical Express responded by raising an action against (i) the landlords and (ii) Vision Express, seeking (a) declarator that the landlords were bound by the terms of the back letter (b) reduction of the lease to Vision Express and (c) interdict, and interim interdict, against Vision Express from trading as opticians from Unit 56. The present case, *Optical Express (Gyle) Ltd* v *Marks and Spencer plc*,[2] was concerned with the question of interim interdict, and thus did not give final decisions on the points in dispute.[3] But the issues were carefully debated and the opinion of Lord Macfadyen has nearly the status of a final determination.

The pursuers were in an awkward position. They perhaps had rights against the now-dissolved District Council. In this action what the pursuers wanted was to show that two *other* parties were bound by the provisions of the back letter, namely the new landlords and Vision Express. Evidently it was not going to be straightforward to establish either point. The new landlords were singular successors of the District Council, and so it would be necessary to show that the obligation was one which would transmit against singular successors. Vision Express were not successors of any sort, so pinning liability on them would be particularly difficult.

The case may be analysed as comprising two parts. The first concerned whether the new landlords were bound. The second was whether Vision Express were bound. The answer to the second question depended largely but not wholly on the answer to the first. For if the new landlords were not bound then the case against Vision Express would be bound to fail. But the converse would not follow: it would be possible for the pursuers to succeed against the new landlords while failing against Vision Express.

The question of what terms of a lease are binding against singular successors is one of considerable difficulty. In Roman law, a lease was simply a contract and not also a real right. Hence, singular successors were not bound by leases granted by their predecessors, unless of course they so agreed (as in practice commonly happened).[4] The Roman rule was, naturally enough, received into our common law, and that remained the law until 1449. The Leases Act of that year changed matters. As interpreted in the case law, it declared that a lease was, in most cases at least, a real right in the land, the real right being established by possession. The Leases Act 1449 is still in force. In the 19th and 20th centuries

---

1 In Land Register areas, a long lease becomes real only upon registration (Land Registration (Scotland) Act 1979, s 3(3)), so that the 1449 Act applies only to short leases (plus long leases created before the area switched to the new register).
2 2000 SLT 644.
3 But it is understood that after the decision the pursuers abandoned their action.
4 See R Zimmermann, *Law of Obligations* (1990) chapter 11 for the Civil Law background.

the 1449 Act was supplemented by other statutes enabling a lease to become a real right by registration.[1] Regardless of whether the real right is established by possession or by registration, the landlord's core obligation—to allow the tenant to possess until the ish—binds singular successors. But what of other obligations? Can they bind singular successors? Or, to put it another way, do they have real effect, or only personal effect?[2]

The law is by no means clear. The authorities indicate that for an obligation to bind singular successors of the landlord, it must be (i) part of the lease itself, and not merely some collateral agreement[3] and (ii) a term which is *inter naturalia* of a lease. The meaning of this latter term has received little attention, whether from judges or from commentators.

In *Optical Express* Lord Macfadyen discussed the first issue in detail but ultimately did not decide it. The pursuer's case, in his view, was 'arguable but not very strong'. For what it is worth, we would respectfully suggest that the back letter was indeed no part of the lease and so incapable of real effect. If the 'collateral agreement' rule has any real bite, it should surely bite in a case like this.

On the second issue—whether such an agreement can be considered to be *inter naturalia* of a lease—Lord Macfadyen found for the defenders. Given the paucity of authority on the *inter naturalia* doctrine, and given its practical significance, this decision is important. According to Lord Macfadyen:[4]

> It is clear from *Bisset v Magistrates of Aberdeen*[5] that one factor relevant to determining whether an obligation is *inter naturalia* of the lease will be whether it is one of common occurrence in the particular class of lease, but it seems to me that the authors of both *Gloag on Contract*[6] and *Cameron and Paton on Landlord and Tenant*[7] perhaps go too far in suggesting that that is the only test . . . [T]he matter is primarily a question of the *nature*[8] of the obligation, although evidence of customary practice will assist in making out a case that a particular obligation is *inter naturalia* of a particular class of lease.

In the present case even if it could have been shown that exclusivity agreements were common in retail leases in shopping centres, that would not have been enough, for an exclusivity agreement, regulating as it does the use of *other* property, is not the sort of thing that can be regarded as *inter naturalia* of a lease.

---

1 For the Sasine Register the Registration of Leases (Scotland) Act 1857 and for the Land Register the Land Registration (Scotland) Act 1979.

2 In *Optical Express* the lease was governed by the Leases Act 1449. Whether there is any difference between such a lease and one registered under the Registration of Leases (Scotland) Act 1857 or under the Land Registration (Scotland) Act 1979, is a difficult question which the decision in *Optical Express* does not touch upon. See further S Brymer, 'Enforcing Commercial Lease Terms against Successsor Landlords' (2001) 49 *Greens Property Law Bulletin* 4.

3 It may be added that the question of whether new landlords could be bound by terms of which they were unaware is one which could hardly arise in practice, because of the rule that only obligations in the lease itself are capable of having real effect.

4 2000 SLT 644 at 650G–I.

5 (1898) 1 F 87.

6 Page 234.

7 Page 95.

8 Emphasis added.

If the obligation did not bind the new landlords, it could hardly bind Vision Express either, and perhaps matters could have been dropped at that point. But the case nevertheless has a valuable discussion of what is often called the 'offside goals' rule.[1] The classic example is *Rodger (Builders) Limited v Fawdry*.[2] Here X sold on missives first to Y and then to Z. X then disponed to Z. Y successfully reduced Z's title on the ground that Z was in bad faith. But the case law, taken as a whole, does not say that *any* disappointed pursuer can reduce the offending right of a bad faith third party. The offside goals rule has its restrictions. In particular, the pursuer's defeated right must have been a right 'capable of being made real'. That being so, the pursuers were doomed to fail. They may have had a personal right limiting the use of the other units in the Centre. But that right was not a right capable of becoming a real right. Hence, it was not protected by the offside goals rule. The decision seems correct in law, as well as making commercial sense.[3]

The question of which terms of a lease will bind successors of the landlord is not always given the attention it deserves. For example, it is not uncommon for a lease to contain an option to purchase. Does that bind singular successors? Surprisingly, the law is unsettled. *Bisset v Magistrates of Aberdeen*[4] held that it does not. But that case was unsatisfactory in a number of respects, and was distinguished in a modern sheriff court decision, *Davidson v Zani*.[5] *Optical Express* leaves that particular question open, but none the less it is of value in consolidating the basic framework, and also as a reminder of the mass of pitfalls in this area.

With the benefit of hindsight, what might Optical Express have done to protect their position? More generally, what should a tenant do to ensure that future landlords will be bound, whether by an exclusivity clause or by some other clause? The modern tendency for commercial leases to be of shorter duration means that this issue is not quite as important as it used to be, but important it still is. One precaution is to ensure that any clause is in the lease itself: the use of a back letter is dangerous. But in *Optical Express* even a clause in the lease would have been insufficient. One step which is sometimes taken is for landlords to bind themselves to ensure that singular successors will also be bound. Probably this is worth doing, but it is doubtful how much it really helps. It is unlikely to be of much help if the landlords go into liquidation or receivership; and if the landlords stay solvent, such a clause may not impose any higher liability than they would have had anyway. The following chart sets out the possibilities. It is presupposed that the old landlords will be liable in damages if the new landlords are entitled to disregard the clause, and do so disregard it.

---

1 For analysis of this doctrine see K G C Reid, *The Law of Property in Scotland* (1996) para 695 *et seq.*
2 1950 SC 483.
3 A J M Steven, 'Keeping the Goalposts in Sight' 2000 SLT (News) 143.
4 (1898) 1 F 87
5 1992 SCLR 1001. This decision—the soundness of which is uncertain—is not mentioned in Lord Macfadyen's opinion.

	Original landlords obliged to ensure new landlords are bound	Original landlords not obliged to ensure new landlords are bound
New landlords bound to honour agreement	Tenants' position satisfactory	Tenants' position satisfactory
New landlords not bound to honour agreement	Tenants have damages claim against old landlords	Tenants have damages claim against old landlords

So the steps so far mentioned are sensible but may be insufficient. What else can be done? The answer seems to be: not much. In principle the obligations incumbent on the landlords could be secured, by third-party guarantee or by a standard security or floating charge, but in practice landlords are unlikely to agree. Moreover, such security will only ensure that any damages will ultimately be paid, whereas tenants will often wish to have the option of interdict, for the practical reason that damages, even if paid in full, are not always a sufficient remedy.

Optical Express draws attention to the point that, in drafting leases, one must always ask whether a particular right will bind successors of the other party. But there is a parallel question which must be kept in view, which is whether a particular right will enure to the benefit of successors of the benefited party. In old-fashioned terminology, the former is the question of passive transmissibility (transmissibility of the liability) while the latter is the question of active transmissibility (transmissibility of the right). Active transmissibility is the subject of the next case.

Rent guarantees: do they transmit?

In *Waydale Ltd* v *DHL Holdings (UK) Ltd (No 2)*[1] the Scottish Development Agency owned industrial property at Bothwellpark in Uddingston and leased it to Elan International Ltd for 20 years from 1987. Elan was a subsidiary of a company called DHL Holdings Ltd, and the SDA insisted that DHL should grant a guarantee for the rent, and DHL agreed to do so. In fact DHL actually granted two guarantees, in similar terms. One was dated and the other not. In 1993 Scottish Enterprise—statutory successors of the SDA—feued the property to Waydale Ltd. In 1994 Elan went into liquidation and stopped paying the rent. Waydale called on DHL to honour their guarantee, and the question was therefore whether the guarantee was only for the benefit of the SDA or whether it enured to the benefit of their successors.

---

1 2001 SLT 224.

The case has been procedurally complex, and so a few words are desirable to set the scene. Waydale first of all raised an action against DHL under the dated guarantee. In 1995 Lord Penrose found in favour of DHL, on the two grounds that the guarantee was not assignable and that even if it had been assignable it had never been assigned.[1] Waydale reclaimed, but later abandoned their appeal. They then raised a new action based on the other guarantee, the undated one, having by this time obtained an assignation of it from the SDA.[2] DHL pled *res judicata*. This plea was repelled by Lord Hamilton.[3] DHL reclaimed, and on 15 December 1999 the Inner House upheld Lord Hamilton's decision on the *res judicata* point.[4] The case thus went back to Lord Hamilton in the Outer House to be determined on the merits, which happened on 20 November 2000.[5] Here is the guarantee which was the basis of the second action:

> We, DHL Holdings (UK) LIMITED . . . hereby guarantee (a) the payment of the rent and all other sums due and owing or to become due or owing in terms of the missives and lease to follow thereon between the Scottish Development Agency, 120 Bothwell Street, Glasgow G2 7JP ('the Agency') and Elan International Limited incorporated under the Companies Acts and having their registered office at Park Lane, Castle Vale, Birmingham ('the tenants') relative to the site and factory premises known as and forming Block 6, Bothwellpark Industrial Estate, Uddingston, dated said missives 5th May and subsequent date(s) all in the year nineteen hundred and eighty seven (b) the performance of all other obligations incumbent upon the tenants in terms of the said missives and lease. In the event of the tenants failing to make payment of rent or of any of the sums of money referred to in the said missives and lease or failing to implement any of the other obligations incumbent on them in terms of the said missives and lease we shall, if requested in writing by the Agency to do, forthwith liquidate the amount due by the tenants and/or implement the outstanding obligations of said missives and lease. This guarantee will subsist in full force and effect notwithstanding that the Agency may have permitted the tenants to delay payment of rent or the implementation of any outstanding obligations incumbent upon them in terms of said missives and lease and we declare that the Agency may enter into any arrangement with the tenants in connection with the said missives and lease without in any way prejudicing their rights against us hereunder. This guarantee will subsist in full force and effect until we have implemented these presents to the satisfaction of the Agency . . .

The guarantee could have been stated to be for the benefit of the landlords as such, or, on the other hand, for the benefit of the SDA alone. But as it was the drafting left everything open. In a case of this sort it would be difficult to say that there is a right answer. It is a matter of impression. The impression of Lord

---

1 *Waydale Ltd v DHL Holdings (UK) Ltd* 1996 SCLR 391.
2 Presumably the later of the two guarantees novated the first. An obligation is discharged by novation. One would guess that the undated guarantee was the earlier of the two, and there is some evidence that this was in fact so. Hence one would imagine that the undated guarantee was discharged. However, this defence does not seem to have been pled by DHL.
3 *Waydale Ltd v DHL Holdings (UK) Ltd* 1999 SLT 631, 1999 SCLR 23. This side of the case is interesting, but not to conveyancers: hence nothing will be said about it here.
4 2001 SLT 207.
5 *Waydale Ltd v DHL Holdings (UK) Ltd (No 2)* 2001 SLT 224.

Hamilton was that the guarantee was intended to benefit the landlord for the time being. The main reason for that conclusion seems to have been that it is the one that makes the best commercial sense. The fact that whereas the tenants are referred to as the 'tenants' the landlords are referred to as the 'Agency' did not carry much weight with him. Nor did the authorities, which say that, in case of ambiguity, a guarantee is to be construed in favour of the guarantor personally.[1]

Lord Hamilton held that the guarantee fell to be construed as enuring directly to the benefit of succeeding landlords even without the need for assignation. Presumably the basis for that is *jus quaesitum tertio*, though that is never spelled out. The point is of some importance. Interestingly, the conclusion arrived at by Lord Hamilton is different from that arrived at, five years ago, by Lord Penrose, on the basis of the dated guarantee.[2] The reason for the different result is not clear. For what it is worth, our own impression is that the guarantee was intended to be personal to the Agency.

The moral of the case is that in drafting leases, and agreements connected with leases, it is important to consider what is to happen should there be a change of parties. The longer the lease the more important this is. It might be pointed out that the guarantee in *Waydale* not only did not make provision for change of landlords but it did not make provision for change of tenants either.

Leases to partnerships—again

The law of leases is often problematic. The same is true of much of the law of partnership. Put the two together and the result is often not a happy one. *Knapdale (Nominees) Ltd v Donald*[3] is a case in point.

In 1935 the farm of Ballochmorrie and Drumgrier at Drumgrier in Ayrshire was let by John Henderson to Robert Donald. Eventually Robert Donald took his son, Robert Donald (junior), into partnership with him, the firm name being Robert Donald & Son. In 1993 another son, Iain Donald, was taken into the partnership. There was no assignation of the lease by Robert (senior) in favour of the firm. Robert (senior) died in 1996. His executors transferred the lease to Robert (junior) in conformity with s 16 of the Succession (Scotland) Act 1964. The original duration of the lease is unclear, but is of little importance, since the tenancy was protected by the Agricultural Holdings (Scotland) Acts 1949 and 1991.

The landlords, Knapdale (Nominees) Ltd, who had acquired ownership of the farm in 1992,[4] raised an action for declarator that there was now no lease and that accordingly they, the landlords, were entitled to vacant possession.

---

1 Nor by the statement in Bell, *Commentaries* I, 392: 'Guarantees and letters of credit are limited to the persons to whom they are addressed, in whose discretion the writer is presumed to have peculiar confidence.'

2 1996 SCLR 391.

3 2000 GWD 19–730.

4 The disposition in favour of Knapdale was recorded GRS Ayr on 7 April 1992. It was executed on 30 September and 7 and 8 October 1991. The date of entry was stated as being 8 June 1987 'notwithstanding the date or dates hereof'. Nothing in the litigation turned on these dates, but we mention them because they are unusual. It perhaps need not be observed that the principle that no real right passes before recording or registration is unaffected by a retrospective date of entry.

The basis of their argument was that Robert (senior) had impliedly renounced the lease, that a new lease had been impliedly constituted in favour of the firm of Robert Donald & Son, and that that firm having been dissolved by the death of Robert (senior) in 1996, the lease came to an end at that time. The factual basis of the argument was that after the partnership was formed the rent began to be paid by the partnership, and latterly rent notices were sent to the partnership rather than to Robert (senior). There were also a number of other bits of evidence suggesting that it was the firm rather than Robert (senior) which had taken over the lease. An important element in the argument from the legal angle was *Morrison-Low* v *Paterson*[1] in which it was held that if there is a lease to a partnership, and the partnership is dissolved and replaced by a successor partnership, and the rent continues to be tendered and accepted, then the successor partnership is deemed to be the new tenant.[2]

Lady Paton held that the facts did not amount to implied renunciation. The decision is of considerable importance, for constellations of facts similar to *Knapdale* must be common in practice. Indeed, one suspects that, had the decision gone the other way, something of a crisis would have ensued. And whilst the decision was based on the particular facts, it may be that in practice few landlords would be able to present a stronger case.

One argument for the defenders was that the lease was with 'the house', which is to say a lease to the firm however constituted. This idea of a 'house' is brought up every time a dispute of this sort reaches the courts. Although judges are happy to say that the doctrine exists, they have a pronounced tendency to ignore it in practice, and *Knapdale* is no exception, Lady Paton saying that if she had not already found in favour of the defenders she would not have found in their favour on this line of argument.

Death of a lessee

What happens when a lessee dies? Does the lease die too? Or does it pass to someone? If so, to whom? This issue is, as with so much in law, best understood historically. Before the Succession (Scotland) Act 1964 a lease would normally pass to the lessee's heir at law, unless both (i) the lease was assignable and (ii) the lessee bequeathed it. But the 1964 Act did away with heirs at law, and so a new system had to be devised. Where a lease would, before 1964, have passed to the heir, since 1964 it has passed to one of a narrow class of persons, defined by s 16 of the 1964 Act as 'any one of the persons entitled to succeed to the deceased's intestate estate, or to claim legal rights or . . . prior rights'. It is the executor who chooses which person in this class to transfer to. (Naturally, the lease should first be confirmed to.) One twist is where the lease has an exclusion of assignation which is implied rather than express. In that case the lessee has a limited power of bequest, namely to anyone in a narrow class, though

---

1 1985 SC (HL) 49.
2 The issue will tend to be important only if the lease is a non-assignable one. See further *Conveyancing 1999* pp 44–48.

apparently not quite the same narrow class.[1] The following tables summarise the position.[2]

Before 1964

	Express prohibition of assignation	Implied prohibition of assignation	Assignation allowed
Testacy	To heir	To heir	To legatee
Intestacy	To heir	To heir	To heir

Since 1964

	Express prohibition of assignation	Implied prohibition of assignation	Assignation allowed
Testacy	Executors can transfer to any member of a narrow class	To legatee, but only if member of a narrow class	To legatee
Intestacy	Executors can transfer to any member of a narrow class	Executors can transfer to any member of a narrow class	Executors can transfer to any member of a narrow class

In the four cases where the executors can transfer to any member of the narrow defined class, there is a time limit. The transfer must be done within a year,[3] which failing either the landlord or the executor can terminate the lease.

In *Sproat* v *South West Services (Galloway) Ltd*[4] an ambiguity in s 16 came into focus. The facts of the case were complex and in some respects obscure. In brief

---

1　1964 Act, s 29. It is curious that the definition of the class is different from the one in s 16. It is 'any one of the persons who, if the tenant had died intestate, would be, or would in any circumstances have been, entitled to succeed to his intestate estate . . .' One of the odd aspects of this definition is that it includes every living person on our planet, for all human beings are related, and so everyone is (under some imaginable 'circumstances') the *haeres ab intestato* of everyone else. By contrast, the class defined in s 16 is limited to direct potential intestate successors. That is reasonably clear from the wording and was confirmed by *MacLean* v *MacLean* 1988 SLT 626.

2　See generally M C Meston, *The Succession (Scotland) Act 1964* (4th edn, 1993).

3　Within one year of what? The section does not say but presumably it means within one year of the death rather than, say, one year of the confirmation. It may be added that the period can be extended by mutual consent, and also, on application of one of the parties, by the sheriff.

4　2000 GWD 37–1416.

there were four long non-assignable leases of adjacent property at Baldoon in Wigtownshire. These leases had been held by John Wyllie, who traded as an agricultural merchant under the name of South West Services. Wyllie died in 1978, and his widow was his universal legatee. In 1979 she confirmed to his estate, including the leases. She continued to trade.[1] Eventually, in 1981, she transferred the leases to herself[2] and in 1994 she assigned them[3] to South West Services (Galloway) Ltd, a company of which she was the majority shareholder. Although she was within the class of persons who could succeed to these leases, the transfers were more than a year after her husband's death. In 1998 the landlord decided to exercise his right to terminate the leases on the ground that there had been no timeous transfer. One defence was that on a proper construction of s 16 of the Succession (Scotland) Act 1964, the executor can carry out the transfer at any time before the landlord terminates the lease, and once the transfer has happened termination is no longer possible. On this view, once the year has passed there is a sort of race, and whoever acts first wins.

There is much to be said in favour of this construction of s 16. However, *dicta* in previous cases[4] had suggested a different construction, namely that the transfer can happen only during the one-year period. The Lord Ordinary (temporary judge T G Coutts QC) chose to follow the earlier *dicta* and repelled the defence. The transfers, having been outwith the one-year period, were void.

Even if they had not been void, the further assignations to the company would have been invalid in view of the non-assignability clauses of the leases themselves. The defenders sought to argue that the landlords, having accepted the position for 20 years, were now barred from seeking to recover possession. They must be regarded as having accepted the company as the tenant for the balance of the 99 years. This argument was rejected. The Lord Ordinary agreed that the pursuer must be regarded as having accepted the company as tenant.[5] But he saw no reason to hold that they were tenants under the original leases. The law is that where a *de facto* lease arises it is regarded as a lease for 12 months, capable of renewal by tacit relocation. Hence the defenders could be required to flit at the end of the current year.

Remarkably, *Sproat* was not the only case in 2000 in which there was a failure to comply with s 16 of the Succession (Scotland) Act 1964. In *Paul v Ogilvy*[6] the non-compliance led to an expensive damages claim against the solicitor involved. It may be that s 16 is not as widely known as it should be, and the problem is all

---

1 It appears that at some stage before his death Mr Wyllie took his wife and son-in-law into partnership with him, and it seems to have been this partnership which continued to trade until the incorporation of South West Services (Galloway) Ltd.

2 Apparently by docket transfer and not by recorded assignation. One of the numerous puzzling features of this case is that she seems to have claimed two of the leases as legatee and the other two by way of prior rights. But prior rights arise only in intestacy.

3 Or perhaps only two of them: we are unclear on this point. The assignations were recorded in the Register of Sasines.

4 *Lord Rotherwick's Trustees* v *Hope* 1975 SLT 187 and *Gifford* v *Buchanan* 1983 SLT 613. These decisions were not conclusive in themselves because their facts were distinguishable.

5 1985 SC (HL) 49.

6 2000 GWD 5–176.

the greater as a result of the decision in *Sproat* that, once the one-year period has passed, the position cannot be retrieved.

Irritancy

In *Euro Properties Scotland Ltd* v *Alam*,[1] the pursuers were the owners of a listed building in Glasgow (the old Britannia Music Hall at 117–119 Trongate). The defenders were the tenants. The lease was for 21 years from 1994 at £120,000 per annum, with quinquennial rent review from 16 May 1994. There were the usual repairing obligations and irritancy provisions. In May 1997 Glasgow City Council served a listed buildings repair notice. Little happened in response, though in 1998 certain public-spirited individuals set up the Britannia Panopticon Music Hall Trust. In December 1998 the landlords served a notice on the tenants specifying a timetable for carrying out the required renovations which failing they would irritate. The timetable called for completion of the renovations within 60 days of the notice. The tenants did not comply. The landlords purported to irritate the lease. When the tenants did not move out, the landlords raised an action for declarator of irritancy, removing and damages of £316,075. The tenants pled in their defence s 5 of the Law Reform (Miscellaneous Provisions) (Scotland) Act 1985, whereby an irritancy is enforceable only if it would be enforced by a 'fair and reasonable landlord'. In making that judgment, the Act directs that 'regard shall be had to whether a reasonable opportunity has been afforded to the tenant to enable the breach to be remedied'.

It was held, after proof, that the landlords were not entitled to irritancy. In the first place, the timetable was impossible to comply with. The fact that the tenants may have dragged their feet at an earlier stage did not justify the imposition of impossible deadlines. In the second place, the lease provided that repairs could be done by the landlords, with the right to recover the cost from the tenants, and in the circumstances that would have been the more reasonable course for the landlords to have taken.

The opinion of Lord Macfadyen contains some interesting *dicta* which will be more welcome to tenants than to landlords: 'Irritancy for failure to implement repair obligations is a course rarely adopted by fair and reasonable landlords.' And again:

It is not *prima facie* fair and reasonable to opt for irritancy when there is available an alternative remedy (by way of the landlord carrying out the repairs and obtaining from the tenant reimbursement of the costs of doing so) which would (a) not deprive the tenant of his interest in the lease but (b) nevertheless adequately protect the landlord's interests.

Lord Macfadyen also retreated somewhat from his own decision in *Aubrey Investments Limited* v *DSC (Realisations) Limited*[2] that the question of what a fair and reasonable landlord would or would not have done falls to be determined at

1 2000 GWD 23–895.
2 1999 SC 21.

the time of the irritancy and that later events are irrelevant. In the *Euro* case he said:

> It seems to me to be conceivable that there could be a case in which it could be affirmed that, at the date of the irritancy notice, a fair and reasonable landlord would rely on the irritancy, but in which before the court reached a decision on the matter further events had taken place which would have led a fair and reasonable landlord to change his mind and decline to rely on the irritancy. The matter is not closed, it seems to me, until the court has granted or refused declarator of irritancy.

The Scottish Law Commission is currently reviewing the provisions in the Law Reform (Miscellaneous Provisions) (Scotland) Act 1985 about irritancy.[1]

Keep-open clauses

During the 1990s the Scottish and English legal systems were hit by a hurricane called 'keep-open clauses'. Where the lease was of a unit in a shopping centre, the lease would typically contain a clause binding the tenant not merely to pay the rent but actually to trade. The reason for such clauses is evident. The viability of a shopping centre depends on a high occupancy rate, and the owners will be particularly keen to ensure that certain facilities are available to shoppers, such as a supermarket, a pharmacy and so on.

The legal problem concerns enforcement in the event of breach. Damages may not be an ideal remedy. They are slow. They may be inadequate, for the award of damages may well not reflect the total negative impact on the centre. Hence landlords wish to be able to enforce by interdict (against proposed breach) plus specific implement. Such orders, if obeyed, will resolve the problem completely—and also rapidly, for such orders are available on the dependence of an action.

Highland and Universal Properties Ltd v *Safeway Properties Ltd*[2] is the latest decision, and may prove to be the definitive one. Amongst all the cases on this subject, the present one has, during its five years before the courts, dominated the scene, and it is fitting that it should have had the benefit of exceptionally care consideration in the Inner House.

Safeways were the anchor tenants of a unit in what used to be called the Wester Hailes Shopping Centre (on the outskirts of Edinburgh), but which is now called the Westside Plaza. They were trading under their 'Presto' name. The lease provided:

> 12. (a) The Lessee undertakes that at all times during the term it will (i) keep the premises open for the trade specified in sub-clause 13(a) herein throughout normal hours of business (ii) use its best endeavours to promote and extend the said trade (iii) maintain at all times an attractive display and (iv) keep the shop for trading and for no other purpose.

---

1 Scottish Law Commission, *Sixth Programme of Law Reform* (Scot Law Com No 176) paras 2.5–2.8.
2 2000 SC 297, 2000 SLT 414. For a valuable discussion, see A Smith, 'Keep on Keeping Open' (2000) 4 *Edinburgh Law Review* 336. For the background to the whole issue see the same author's 'Specific Implement' in K Reid and R Zimmermann (eds), *A History of Private Law in Scotland* vol II (2000) .

This was followed by the remarkable clause 13(a):

> 13. (a) Not at any time during the term to use or permit the premises to be used for any illegal immoral noisome noxious dangerous or offensive trade manufacture business or purpose whatsoever nor for the carrying on of anything which shall or may be a nuisance damage annoyance disturbance or inconvenience to the neighbourhood or to the public local or any other authorities or to the Head Lessor, the Lessor or to the tenants or owners or occupiers of adjoining or adjacent premises or which in the opinion of the Lessor shall or may in any way be injurious to the same or be detrimental to the amenity of the development nor set up or permit to be set up in any part of the premises any steam gas oil electric hot air or other engine machine or mechanical contrivance (other than usual shop equipment) nor overload any of the floors or walls or ceilings of the premises or the gas electricity or water supplies or drains connecting therewith nor commit any wilful or voluntary waste or destruction nor deposit any refuse in or upon the premises or any part of the development nor without prejudice to the foregoing generality allow any sale by auction to be held on the premises or any part of the development or permit the premises to be used as a shooting gallery an amusement arcade or a club or operate or permit the operation of pintables therein or reside or sleep or permit anyone to reside or sleep therein or use or suffer or permit the premises to be used otherwise than for the retail sale of all goods which may from time to time be sold in *a high class retail store*[1] including the sale of wines, beers and spirits and the operation of part of the premises for café and restaurant purposes.

In 1995 Safeways decided to pull out, in defiance of their obligations under the lease. In the Outer House the landlords succeeded in obtaining interim orders against them, and these were later made permanent.[2] The present case upholds those decisions.[3]

The specific enforcement of a keep-open clause had already been allowed by another Division of the Inner House in *Retail Parks Investments Ltd* v *Royal Bank of Scotland*,[4] but in that case the competence of such orders was not challenged. Moreover, since *Retail Parks* the House of Lords, in an English case, had refused to grant specific enforcement of a keep-open clause.[5] In *Highland & Universal*, however, the First Division had no hesitation in adhering to the traditional view that Scots and English law differ in their approach to the specific enforcement of contracts. In English law specific enforcement is not normally allowed, special cases apart. In Scots law the reverse is true: specific enforcement is the rule, and is refused only in special cases.[6] (Of course, in practice the difference between the two systems is not so great, since pursuers in contract cases often do not

---

1 Emphasis added.
2 1996 SLT 559 and 1998 GWD 3–136.
3 Strictly the decision of the Lord Ordinary was reversed, but only on a detail as to the wording of the decree. In substance the decision was sustained.
4 1996 SC 227.
5 *Co-operative Insurance* v *Argyll Stores Ltd* [1998] AC 1.
6 One is here considering only non-pecuniary obligations. A decree of specific implement for the payment of money is incompetent, and the same is true in other legal systems, including English law. A decree for payment is not regarded as a decree *ad factum praestandum* and enforcement is by means of diligence, sequestration or liquidation.

want specific enforcement anyway, and so do not ask for it.) Hence, English authority on keep-open clauses is only of limited significance.

The relationship between owner and sub-tenant

Suppose a lessee wants to sub-let, but this requires the landlord's consent. The landlord is happy to agree, provided that the sub-lease contains a clause whereby assignations of the sub-lease will require the consent of the head landlord. And suppose that the sub-lease is granted in those terms. Can the sub-tenant assign without the head landlord's consent?

The question may seem absurd. 'Of course not' is the obvious answer. But the situation may not be so simple. In *Sears Properties Netherlands BV v Coal Pension Properties Ltd*[1] a sub-lease contained the following clause, inserted as required by the head landlords:

> Not to assign or sub-let the whole of the sub-tenant's interest in the whole of the Premises without previously obtaining the written consent of the Landlord and the Mid-Landlord (which consent shall not be unreasonably withheld in the case of the Mid-Landlord to a proposed assignee or sub-tenant who is respectable and responsible and demonstrably capable of performing the sub-tenant's full obligations under the Sub-lease) and provided that it shall be a condition precedent to the grant of any such consent that the sub-tenant shall at its own expense if required by the Mid-Landlord procure a written undertaking in favour of the Mid-Landlord and the Landlord in a form approved by them by any permitted assignee or Sub-tenant to observe and perform the obligations of the sub-tenant and the conditions herein contained and (except in the case of the Sub-tenant) an obligation for the payment of the rents and other sums stipulated in the Sub-lease including an undertaking in the same terms *mutatis mutandis* as in this sub-clause (e) and subject to like proviso.

The mid-landlords sought declarator that the head landlords were not entitled to refuse consent to an assignation of the sub-lease. Declarator was granted as concluded for. Naturally the head landlords pled *jus quaesitum tertio*, but this plea was rejected. Why? One reason was reliance on a House of Lords case dating from 1835, *Duke of Queensberry's Executors v Maxwell*,[2] the *ratio* of which was, in the words of the House of Lords itself, 'there being no privity of contract between [lessor and sub-lessee] no rights or obligations can arise directly between them on the footing of contract'. With respect, however, that decision is of questionable value. In that case, a lease was reduced, and the sub-lessee, who thereby lost his sub-lease, sued the head landlord in warrandice. Whether the warrandice granted in the principal lease enured to the benefit of the sub-lessee was a difficult question. The Whole Court decided, by a majority, in favour of the sub-lessee. This was reversed by an English judge sitting alone in the House of Lords. Now, one may have an interesting academic debate as to the respective weight of authority as between the Whole Court on the one hand

---

1 2000 SCLR 1002. The head lease was for the period from 1996 to 2095.
2 (1831) 5 W & Sh 771.

and a single English judge on the other, on a point which was not one of the construction of a UK statute but of Scots common law. But that debate need not be entered into here. The judge concerned made no attempt to apply Scots law, but instead decided the case according to the English doctrine of privity. The idea that there *cannot* be direct obligations between head-landlord and sub-lessee is simply untrue.

But it may be that the respect shown to *Duke of Queensberry's Executors* v *Maxwell* was no more than lip-service, for the Lord Ordinary (Eassie) in fact did not dismiss the possibility of *jus quaesitum tertio* out of hand. The Lord Ordinary effectively agreed that a *jus quaesitum tertio* could arise between head landlord and sub-lessee, and he weighed the arguments as to whether it existed on the facts of the case. His decision that it did not exist is perhaps debatable. In favour of that decision it could be said that the head landlord's consent was merely a condition, which did not confer any positive rights on the head landlord.

Whether the decision was right or wrong, it points to a moral. If a contract between A and B is to confer rights on C, that needs to be made very clear. Although privity is no part of Scots law in the sense of being a strict doctrine, it is part of the law in the sense of a presumption, and it takes clear intentions to overcome that presumption. With the benefit of hindsight the head landlords would have insisted on a differently-worded clause.

REAL BURDENS

Validity of clause providing for appointment of factors

Principles
It has always been common in the west of Scotland, and is increasingly common elsewhere, to make provision in titles for the appointment of a factor (or property manager, to use a more modern term). Factors are generally found in tenements, and in other developments with shared facilities. Roughly speaking, the provision usually takes one of three possible forms:

(i) the factor is to be appointed by the owners of a majority of the flats (or other units);

(ii) the factor is to be appointed by the developer, for as long as the developer owns a stipulated number of units in the development (often one is enough); thereafter the factor is to be appointed by the owners of a majority of units;

(iii) the factor is to be appointed by the developer in perpetuity.[1]

Type (iii) is rarely found outside sheltered housing developments. Type (ii) is used both by local authorities in the sale of council houses and also by private developers. Type (i) is found in private developments, particularly those built on a relatively small scale.

---

1 There are evidently technical difficulties about title and interest to enforce, but hitherto it has been the practice for the developer to retain the superiority.

In policy terms, type (i) clauses are unobjectionable. Factors are useful (some would say essential), and the principle of majority rule is usually regarded as reasonable. The other types of clause have been more controversial. According to their critics, they tend to confer monopoly powers on the developer/council, leading to high charges and a lack of consultation. A report published in 1999 by the Scottish Consumers Association was critical of the factoring service offered by many councils.[1] But there are also arguments the other way. For as long as a developer is on-site and continuing to sell houses, he has a legitimate interest in the proper factoring of those parts of the estate which have already been sold. For an estate which is badly maintained will be unattractive to purchasers. Moreover, local authorities would argue that there is a public interest in the proper maintenance of developments which contain a mixture of public and private housing. This is not only to protect such housing stock as remains in the public sector but also to help those former tenants who have recently bought their own homes and may be unfamiliar with the obligations arising from private ownership. For cases such as these, a type (ii) clause may seem a reasonable compromise between control and freedom. The developer/authority can appoint a factor for as long as there is a legitimate interest to do so. Thereafter it is for the owners of the units to make their own decisions.

Type (iii) clauses are sometimes justified on the basis that people buy into sheltered housing precisely because they want to be relieved of the burden of self-management. On this view, a factoring system controlled by the developer is a type of social service.

If factoring provisions are to run with the land, they need to be properly constituted as real burdens. There have been thought to be three difficulties with using real burdens for this purpose.

The first difficulty arises out of the rule that a real burden must confer praedial benefit, that is to say, that it must burden one property for the benefit of another. Factoring, undeniably, is capable of creating a benefit, but some have doubted whether the benefit can properly be characterised as praedial.[2]

The next difficulty concerns entrenchment on ownership. The obligation created by a real burden must not be so severe that it is repugnant with ownership. 'You cannot make a man proprietor', according to Lord Young, 'and yet prohibit him from exercising the rights of proprietorship'.[3] One of the fundamental rights of ownership is the right to manage one's own property. A real burden which purports to take this away in perpetuity (as in a type (iii) clause) seems invalid as repugnant with ownership; and even a type (ii) clause might be vulnerable under this head.

The final difficulty is the rule that real burdens must not have the effect of creating a monopoly. That would be contrary to public policy.[4] If a person has a

---

1 Scottish Consumer Council, *In a Fix* (1999).
2 See, *eg* R Rennie, 'The Reality of Real Burdens' 1998 SLT (News) 149 at 149–151.
3 *Moir's Trs v McEwan* (1880) 7 R 1141 at 1145.
4 K G C Reid, *The Law of Property in Scotland* (1996) para 391.

right to force others to use his factorial services, that can readily be characterised as a monopoly.

Litigation

Until recently these issues had not been litigated in the context of factoring. But the validity of factoring arrangements was challenged in *Dumbarton District Council v McLaughlin*.[1] The litigation concerned a 10-unit block of flats at McColl Avenue in Alexandria. Dumbarton District Council sold one of the flats under the right-to-buy legislation, but, for the moment, retained the other nine. The conveyancing was carried out by disposition. The disposition included the following clause (which, in due course, appeared in the land certificate):

> 9. The Council for as long as it may be the proprietor of any dwellinghouse(s) adjoining the subjects or of any dwellinghouse(s) forming part of a larger building of which the subjects form part, shall be entitled to act as common factors or to nominate and appoint factors in respect of the said dwellinghouse(s) and said factors shall, in addition to all normal functions for which the factors may claim normal factorage and expenses be entitled to require all reasonable maintenance and repair to be carried out and any such requisition shall be binding on all proprietors of the dwellinghouse(s) . . . In the event of the Council ceasing to be the proprietors of any of the said dwellinghouse(s), the proprietors thereof shall be entitled to nominate and appoint common factors as aforesaid on a majority basis, each dwellinghouse being one vote and the said factors appointed shall have the same powers as aforementioned.

This is a type (ii) clause. When the Council tried to recover factors' dues of £46.78 against the owner (a successor of the original purchaser), payment was resisted on the ground, among others, that the clause was invalid as creating an unlawful monopoly. This argument was rejected by the sheriff.[2] The clause was not, in the sheriff's view, designed to achieve commercial advantage. It was not like the monopolies expressly disapproved of in *Tailors of Aberdeen v Coutts*[3] —monopolies requiring the owner to use the superiors' brewer or smith. Rather, its purpose was 'to put in place . . . a system for the proper repair and maintenance of the common parts of the tenement'.[4] As such it was lawful.

For several reasons this decision is less useful than it might have been. First, the discussion was confined to the question of monopoly powers, the third of the three arguments mentioned above. There was no consideration of the other two arguments (praedial benefit, and repugnancy with ownership).

Second, even in relation to monopoly powers, there was (understandably) no discussion of different types of factoring clauses. It is good to know that, in the sheriff's opinion, a type (ii) clause is not an unlawful monopoly. But that

---

1 2000 HousLR 16 (Sh Ct). Although only now reported, the case was actually decided in 1996.
2 S W H Fraser.
3 (1840) 1 Rob 296 .
4 2000 HousLR 16 at p 25 (para 25–60).

tells us nothing about type (iii) clauses. Our view would be that such clauses are unlawful.[1]

Finally, the sheriff's opinion was in any event *obiter*. The clause failed for another reason entirely.[2] The right reserved to the Council in clause 9 was a right to factor only 'the said dwellinghouse(s)'; and on closer examination of the clause it was clear that 'the said dwellinghouse(s)' meant the houses retained by the Council and not the house ('the subjects') which had actually been sold. In other words, the clause merely gave to the Council a right which it had anyway, namely to factor its *own* properties. Presumably this is not what was intended by the clause. But in a real burden what matters is what is said rather than what was intended to be said.[3] If nothing else, therefore, the case is an illustration of the importance of reading burdens with a critical eye.

Reform

All three possible objections to factoring clauses are dealt with in the draft Title Conditions (Scotland) Bill, which is included in the Scottish Law Commission's *Report on Real Burdens* (Scot Law Com No 181, 2000).[4]

The objection that such a clause might be insufficiently praedial to constitute a real burden is met by a statement, in s 2(3), that 'a real burden may be created which . . . makes provision for management or administration'.[5]

The principle that a real burden must be neither repugnant with ownership nor have the effect of creating a monopoly is expressly reaffirmed by s 3. In particular s 3(7) provides that:

> Except in so far as expressly permitted by this Act, a real burden must not have the effect of creating a monopoly (as for example, by providing for a particular person to be or to appoint—
>
> (a) the manager of property or
> (b) the supplier of any services in relation to the property).

But what is taken away is then restored, to some extent, by s 53, which allows the creation of 'manager burdens', that is to say, real burdens reserving the right to appoint the manager of a development. Manager burdens, however, are both time-limited and also property-limited. They have a maximum duration of

---

1 A type (iii) clause was litigated in *Sheltered Housing Management Ltd* v *Aitken* (1997), collected in R R M Paisley and D J Cusine (eds), *Unreported Property Cases from the Sheriff Courts* (2000) 225, but the case was eventually decided on a contractual basis, the defender being the first purchaser.
2 It also failed on an issue of interpretation. See below.
3 In theory a defectively expressed burden might be open to judicial rectification under s 8 of the Law Reform (Miscellaneous Provisions) (Scotland) Act 1985, so as to make the wording accord with the original intention. But in practice the possibility would be likely to be barred by the provisions of s 9.
4 For further commentary on this Bill, see below. The Report (which includes the Bill as an appendix) can be viewed at www.scotlawcom.gov.uk
5 And see also (a) s 3(4) which restates the praedial rule for community burdens ('A community burden may be for the benefit of the community to which it relates or of some part of that community'), and (b) s 24(1) which makes clear that community burdens can make provision in relation to decision-making.

10 years—or 30 years in cases involving local authorities or other social landlords selling under the right-to-buy legislation. And they may be exercised only for as long as the person holding the power to appoint the manager owns one of the units in the development. The broad effect of s 53 is to allow type (ii) clauses (subject to a maximum duration of 10/30 years), but to disallow type (iii) clauses. Section 53 applies to all clauses making provision for managers, including those created before the passing of the legislation.

A Bill based on the Scottish Law Commission's draft is expected to be introduced to the Scottish Parliament, following consultation, in the second half of 2001.

Interpretation

Real burdens fall to be interpreted in favour of freedom and against the person seeking to enforce them.[1] The standard applied to real burdens is considerably more rigorous than that which is applied to servitudes.[2] Two cases from the most recent crop emphasise once again the difficulties facing those who draft real burdens.

Dumbarton District Council v *McLaughlin* has already been mentioned in the context of the enforceability of factoring arrangements. But the clause in question, clause 9 (quoted above), also failed on a point of interpretation. In terms of the clause the Council was entitled to claim 'normal factorage and expenses' in respect of the 'normal functions' of factors. This is not very precise drafting, and it comes as no surprise that the clause was held to be unenforceable on grounds of uncertainty. 'Factorage and expenses' varied from public sector to private sector, and probably from factor to factor. Accordingly, there was no such thing as 'normal' factorage and expenses. In order to burden the land it was necessary to be much more precise.

In *Grampian Joint Police Board* v *Pearson*[3] land at Kirktown of Echt, Aberdeen had been feued in 1901 for the erection of a police house 'with an appropriate number of cells for police purposes'. The Feu Charter provided that, if the house was sold for private use, the superiors were to be entitled to buy it back at a price not greater than 'the original cost of said buildings'. The clause was held to be void from uncertainty, partly because of the difficulty, today, in determining the original cost, and partly because it was unclear whether that cost included architects' and other professional fees. It is possible that these difficulties were exaggerated. If enforced, the burden would have operated oppressively; and it would not be unknown for the rules of strict construction to be used as a means of striking down burdens which were unacceptable on other grounds.[4]

---

1 K G C Reid, *The Law of Property in Scotland* (1996) paras 415 to 422.
2 *cf Conveyancing 1999* pp 57–59.
3 2001 SLT 90.
4 One wonders whether the Police Board was in truth a singular successor. If not, the burden might perhaps have been valid even if not real.

The Title Conditions Bill proposes a shift away from ultra-strict construction. Section 13 provides that: 'Real burdens shall be construed in the same manner as other provisions of deeds which relate to land and are intended for registration.' The effect would be to bring real burdens into line with servitudes. Whether a more relaxed approach would have saved either of the two burdens described above is, however, questionable.

Reform

Introduction

Before the end of 2001 a Bill to reform the law of real burdens—the Title Conditions (Scotland) Bill—is expected to be introduced to the Scottish Parliament. This will be preceded by a consultation period in the spring. Once enacted, some of the Bill's provisions will come into force at once but most will await the day of feudal abolition (still some time in the future). Thus, the intention is that the Abolition of Feudal Tenure etc (Scotland) Act 2000 and the Title Conditions (Scotland) Act should come into force on the same day. A draft of the Bill is already in the public domain, as an appendix to the Scottish Law Commission's *Report on Real Burdens*.[1] A full explanation of the Bill will be found in the Commission's Report. The Bill runs to 119 sections and 9 schedules, and it is possible to offer only the barest summary here.

The name of the Bill requires explanation. 'Title condition' is not, at the moment, a technical term of law. In the Bill, 'title condition' is used as a generic term for real burdens, servitudes, conditions in long leases, and other obligations which are capable of variation or discharge by the Lands Tribunal. Its closest equivalent in the current law is 'land obligation', as used in Part I of the Conveyancing and Feudal Reform (Scotland) Act 1970. The Bill, as its name suggests, contains provisions affecting all title conditions.[2] But overwhelmingly the Bill is about real burdens.

Reasons for reform

The Scottish Law Commission gives a number of reasons for proposing legislation on real burdens. One is the unsatisfactory state of the current law, which in places is confused and incoherent, or needlessly complex.

Another reason is the forthcoming abolition of feudalism, and hence of feudal real burdens. This makes it necessary to recast the law of real burdens in a non-feudal form. At the moment real burdens are often held by superiors. In the future they can—subject to certain exceptions— be held only by neighbours.[3] A non-feudal real burden is like a servitude. There must be both a 'benefited property' and a 'burdened property' (to use the language of the Title Conditions Bill); and the burdens are enforceable by the owner of the former against the

---

1 Scot Law Com No 181. It is available at www.scotlawcom.gov.uk
2 We have already considered provisions of the Bill dealing with servitudes. See pp 55–56.
3 In what follows it is assumed that the Bill will be enacted as it stands. But, of course, that this will be so cannot be taken for granted.

owner of the latter. Non-feudal burdens are perfectly familiar under the present law. Every time a real burden is created in an ordinary disposition, or in a deed of conditions granted in association with such a disposition, it is non-feudal in character. But after feudal abolition all real burdens will be non-feudal.

Then there is the issue of transparency of the registers. At the moment the registers give a very incomplete picture. Even although non-feudal burdens involve two properties, one benefited and one burdened, the law requires registration against the burdened property alone. Of course sometimes, by chance, the burden appears on the title sheet of the benefited property as well. More usually it does not, in which case the person with title to enforce may have no idea of the burden's existence. Worse than this, the identity of the benefited property may actually be unknown. Burdens are often silent on the question of enforcement rights, in which case the position is governed by the complex, and barely workable, rules on implied rights (often referred to as implied *jus quaesitum tertio*). The result is that, while burdened owners are in no doubt of their obligations, they may have no idea who has title to enforce them. If they want a minute of waiver they will not know where to turn.

Finally, there is the issue of longevity. Some real burdens are unaffected by the passage of time and remain as useful today as when first created. Others rapidly become obsolete or inconvenient or, in changed circumstances, unduly restrictive. For the system to work properly, therefore, it is necessary to have adequate means of removing burdens. And the sheer scale on which burdens are used in Scotland—far greater than in other European countries—makes the need all the more pressing. Here the present law falls down. Every conveyancer is familiar with the unauthorised alteration which comes to light the day before settlement. Often the alteration is trivial. It was not objected to at the time, and has not been objected to since. Probably it is an alteration to which no reasonable person would object. Yet the transaction cannot go ahead unless someone can be found to sign a minute of waiver. Here the expense, and trouble, are out of all proportion to the nature of the breach.

A statutory restatement

Part 1 of the Title Conditions Bill (ss 1 to 22) comprises a statutory restatement of the law of real burdens. This means that a person seeking to discover the law will at least know where to begin. The emphasis is on continuity. While the law is changed in places, much of the work of the Bill is clarification and not innovation. Some of the more important changes are mentioned later. The statutory restatement covers all the main stages in the life cycle of real burdens. There are rules on creation (ss 2 to 5), title and interest to enforce (ss 7 to 10), division of the benefited or burdened properties (ss 11 and 12), interpretation (s 13), and extinction (ss 14 to 22). The Bill begins with a definition: in the post-feudal world 'a real burden is an encumbrance on land constituted in favour of the owner of other land in his capacity as owner of that other land'.[1]

---

1 Title Conditions (Scotland) Bill, s 1(1).

Creation of real burdens

The Bill alters the rules about creation of burdens in several ways. At present, real burdens can be created only in a conveyance of the burdened property or in a deed of conditions. That restriction is removed by s 4(2). In future, a real burden can be created in a deed of any kind. Further (and by contrast with the current rule for deeds of conditions), the granter's title need not have been completed by registration, and deduction of title is permitted. But in other ways, the new law is more demanding than the old. The term 'real burden' must be used (or the name of some type of real burden, such as a 'community burden', mentioned below). The deed must nominate and identify the benefited property or properties. It will no longer be possible for enforcement rights to arise by implication. And the deed must be registered not only against the burdened property, as at present, but against the benefited property as well.

Enforcement

Under the Bill real burdens can be enforced, not only by the owner of the benefited property (as at present), but by others holding possessory real rights, most notably tenants.[1] And a real burden can be enforced *against* any occupant of the burdened property.[2] So a tenant, for example, can be prevented from carrying on a business, contrary to the deed of conditions. Affirmative burdens, however—burdens imposing an obligation to do something, such as pay for a repair—can be enforced only against the owner.[3] When property is sold at a time when an affirmative burden is outstanding, the seller remains liable, and the enforcer has a choice of suing either the seller or the buyer.[4]

Division of benefited properties

Superiorities cannot normally be divided. Benefited properties can. Where this occurs there is often an unwelcome proliferation of enforcement rights. If, for example, 100 houses come to be built on the plot of ground which is the benefited property in a real burden, the burden is suddenly enforceable by 100 different people, and minutes of waiver cease to be a practical proposition. Section 11 responds to this problem by providing that, except where the deed says otherwise, any land split off from the original benefited property will lose the status of a benefited property.

Extinction of real burdens

Several provisions in the Bill have the object of making extinction of burdens easier than under the present law. The period of negative prescription is reduced from 20 years to 5.[5] Acquiescence is given statutory status, and it is made clear that it is properly extinctive of burdens, to the extent of the breach acquiesced

---

1 Title Conditions (Scotland) Bill, s 7(2).
2 Title Conditions (Scotland) Bill, s 8(2).
3 Title Conditions (Scotland) Bill, s 8(1).
4 Title Conditions (Scotland) Bill, s 9.
5 Title Conditions (Scotland) Bill, s 16.

in.[1] Further, acquiescence is presumed once the breach is completed. So in the case of an unauthorised alteration, there will be a presumption that the person with enforcement rights did not object at the time and that a challenge is now barred. Part 9 of the Bill reformulates the grounds for variation and discharge of real burdens (and other title conditions) by the Lands Tribunal. If a Tribunal application is unopposed, the application is granted as of right.[2] A person who opposes an application must pay a fee[3] and, if unsuccessful, may be liable for the applicant's expenses.[4] The Tribunal is given a new jurisdiction to determine the validity and effect of real burdens.[5]

An important innovation is a termination procedure for burdens more than 100 years old.[6] Instead of seeking a minute of waiver, the burdened owner can discharge the burdens by serving and registering a notice of termination. The benefited owner's consent is not required. But the notice of termination cannot be registered if, within eight weeks of service, the benefited owner applies to the Lands Tribunal for the burdens to be renewed. In that event, the future of the burden is determined by the Tribunal. Some types of burden are excluded from the termination procedure, the most important being 'facility burdens', that is to say, burdens concerned with the maintenance and regulation of facilities such as the common parts of a tenement or housing estate, or a private road, or a boundary fence. Facility burdens are already familiar (although not by name) from s 23 of the Abolition of Feudal Tenure etc (Scotland) Act 2000.[7] The importance of such burdens is self-evident, and this is one of a number of occasions in which they are singled out for special treatment.

Community burdens

Real burdens can be used to regulate discrete communities, such as housing estates or tenements or sheltered housing developments. If, as often, the burdens are mutually enforceable by the owners of individual units, they are classified by the Title Conditions (Scotland) Bill as 'community burdens'. Part 2 of the Bill makes special provision for such burdens (whether created before or after the Bill). A rudimentary management scheme is introduced which applies where the titles do not otherwise provide. This allows the owners of a majority of units to appoint (or dismiss) a manager/factor,[8] and to instruct common maintenance.[9] In place of the current rule that all owners must concur in a minute of waiver, the new rule is that burdens can be discharged by the owners of a majority of units or, where authorised to do so, by the manager (s 30).[10] At least one near neighbour must also sign.

---

1 Title Conditions (Scotland) Bill, s 15.
2 Title Conditions (Scotland) Bill, s 92.
3 Title Conditions (Scotland) Bill, s 91.
4 Title Conditions (Scotland) Bill, s 95.
5 Title Conditions (Scotland) Bill, s 85(1).
6 Title Conditions (Scotland) Bill, ss 18 to 22.
7 They are defined in s 113 of the Title Conditions Bill.
8 Title Conditions (Scotland) Bill, s 26.
9 Title Conditions (Scotland) Bill, s 27.
10 Title Conditions (Scotland) Bill, s 30.

Development Management Scheme

Part 6 of the Title Conditions (Scotland) Bill introduces an off-the-peg management scheme which can be used, if desired, in new developments such as housing estates. The scheme itself is set out in Schedule 3, and can be applied to a development either in the form enacted or with appropriate changes. Management is in the hands of an owners' association, which is a body corporate (but not a company). All owners are members. The members must meet at least annually in order to approve the accounts for the previous year and the budget for the forthcoming year. It may also meet at other times. Day-to-day management is delegated to a manager, appointed at an annual meeting and advised by an advisory committee of owners.

Burdens without a benefited property

Normally a real burden must have a benefited property. But, following the Abolition of Feudal Tenure etc (Scotland) Act 2000,[1] the Title Conditions (Scotland) Bill makes an exception for conservation burdens and maritime burdens. These are enforceable, respectively, by conservation bodies or the Crown. The relevant provisions are in Part 3. A third exception, manager burdens, was mentioned earlier.[2] Unusually, the relevant provisions of the Bill come into force immediately on Royal Assent, thus allowing new conservation, maritime and manager burdens to be created in advance of feudal abolition.

Transitional: implied rights of enforcement

Mention has been made already of the rules, barely workable in practice, by which a right to enforce real burdens may arise by implication. With one exception, discussed below, all such rights currently in existence are swept away by Part 4 of the Bill.[3] In their place come new statutory rights. By a provision modelled on s 23 of the Feudal Act, facility burdens are in future to be enforceable by the owners of those properties taking benefit from the facility in question.[4] Real burdens imposed under a common scheme on all the flats in a tenement are to be enforceable by the owners of each flat.[5] A similar rule is applied to sheltered housing.[6] In other cases of burdens imposed under a common scheme—in housing estates, for example—enforcement rights are restricted to close neighbours, defined as those owning property within four metres, discounting roads (s 44).[7] But, like the rules being replaced, enforcement rights arise only if the existence of the common scheme is clear from the deed imposing the burdens, and if there is nothing in that deed inconsistent with the idea of enforcement rights being held by neighbours. The standard example of inconsistency is the provision, often found in deeds of conditions, by which the

---

1 Abolition of Feudal Tenure etc (Scotland) Act 2000, ss 26 to 32 and 60.
2 The relevant provision is s 53.
3 Title Conditions (Scotland) Bill, s 41.
4 Title Conditions (Scotland) Bill, s 47. For s 23 see pp 129–130.
5 Title Conditions (Scotland) Bill, s 45.
6 Title Conditions (Scotland) Bill, s 46.
7 Title Conditions (Scotland) Bill, s 44, read with s 116.

granter reserves the right to vary the burdens. The provisions just described are transitional. They have no application to real burdens created after the Bill comes into force. In the case of new burdens, as already mentioned, the benefited properties must be identified in the deed.

In one case existing implied rights are not swept away, or at least not at once. In *J A Mactaggart & Co* v *Harrower*[1] it was held that, where A dispones to B imposing real burdens but retaining other land in the neighbourhood, the burdens are enforceable by A and his successors as owners of the retained land.[2] There is no common scheme in a case like this, or at any rate the retained land is unaffected by such a scheme. The Title Conditions (Scotland) Bill allows enforcement rights implied under this rule to be preserved by registration of a statutory notice within a period of 10 years.[3] Any rights not preserved in this way are then extinguished at the end of 10 years.[4]

School Sites Act 1841
Former schools are sometimes vulnerable to the statutory reversion created by the third proviso to s 2 of the School Sites Act. That reversion is triggered as soon as the building ceases to be used as a school. Nonetheless, in practice these former schools have often been sold by the education authority to private purchasers. The Bill gives protection to such purchasers and their successors.[5] The reversion itself is extinguished, and the reversion-holder[6] has instead a claim against the relevant education authority for the free proceeds of sale (less the value of improvements). If the site has remained the property of the authority, the reversion-holder can seek a reconveyance (on payment of the value of improvements) or its value.

Other topics
Other topics touched on by the Title Conditions (Scotland) Bill include rights of pre-emption and redemption,[7] and the effect of compulsory purchase on real burdens and servitudes.[8] The rules about ranking of standard securities are adjusted to accommodate clawback arrangements.[9]

---

1 (1906) 8 F 1101. See further K G C Reid, *The Law of Property in Scotland* (1996) paras 403 and 404.
2 For a challenge to this doctrine, see *Marsden* v *Craighelen Lawn Tennis and Squash Club* 1999 GWD 37–1820, discussed at pp 59–61 of *Conveyancing 1999*.
3 Title Conditions (Scotland) Bill, s 42.
4 Title Conditions (Scotland) Bill, s 41.
5 Title Conditions (Scotland) Bill, s 82.
6 It is not settled whether the reversion-holder is the universal or the singular successor of the original granter of the site—or in other words, whether the reversion is personal or praedial. See para 10.47 of the *Report on Real Burdens*. The most recent case, from the Court of Appeal in England and decided after the publication of the *Report*, suggests that it is personal. See *Fraser and Another* v *Canterbury Diocesan Board of Finance*, *The Times* 10 January 2001, [2001] TLR 22.
7 Title Conditions (Scotland) Bill, ss 78 to 80.
8 Title Conditions (Scotland) Bill, ss 98 to 100.
9 Title Conditions (Scotland) Bill, s 102.

STANDARD SECURITIES AND FLOATING CHARGES

Priority as between floating charges and standard securities

Nowadays it is a truism, not merely among academics but more recently among the judiciary too, that the floating charge is an 'alien' conception, a conception which does not fit in readily with the general fabric of Scots law. Its essentially alien nature is not ameliorated by provisions in the 1985 Companies Act of an obscurity which is noteworthy even by the standards of the Westminster statute book.

Section 464 contains provisions about the ranking of floating charges, including their interaction with ordinary securities such as standard securities. The basic rule is that a floating charge ranks not from the date of its creation but from the date of its attachment, or crystallisation. Thus, if ABC Ltd grants a floating charge to DEF Bank in year 1, and grants a standard security to GHI Bank in year 2, and goes into receivership in year 3, the standard security, though created later, ranks first. That may seem surprising, but that is what the section says.[1]

But the section then proceeds to establish exceptions (and, indeed, exceptions to the exceptions). The most important exception is that the floating charge can itself contain a clause, sometimes known as a negative pledge clause, which reverses the basic rule, and imposes a *prior tempore potior jure* rule. Not surprisingly, floating charges in practice almost always contain such a clause.

Bank of Ireland v *Bass Brewers*[2] has a complex history. Lewis Lloyd Holdings Ltd granted a variety of securities to a variety of different lenders. For present purposes only two are important, namely a floating charge to Bass, and a later standard security to the Bank of Ireland over property at Hazelburn, Campbeltown.

The floating charge in favour of Bass was granted:

> over the whole of the property which is or may be from time to time while this security is in force comprised in our property and undertaking but so that we are hereby and shall be prohibited from creating subsequent to our execution hereof any fixed security within the meaning of subsection (1) of section 70 of the Insolvency Act 1986 or any statutory amendment or re-enactment thereof for the time being in force having priority over or ranking equally with the Floating Charge hereby created save as specified in the Schedule contained herein and save in favour of the Company [= Bass] . . .

And the borrowers (Lewis Lloyd Holdings Ltd) agreed:

> Unless with the written consent of the Company [= Bass] we shall not create or allow to come into being any security or charge upon any part of the property (including heritable, real and leasehold property wherever situated) assets undertaking or uncalled capital of us or any of our subsidiary companies . . .

---

1 Actually, there is a logic here. A floating charge only becomes a real right as and when it attaches.
2 2000 GWD 28–1077.

When the standard security was granted Bass wrote to the Bank of Ireland:

> We confirm that we have no intention of appointing a receiver under the floating charge granted by Lewis Lloyd Holdings Ltd and will not do so within the next 21 days. We consent to the granting of Standard Securities by Lewis Lloyd Holdings Ltd in favour of the Governor and Company of the Bank of Ireland ... over the subjects.

It is not difficult to see that this consent was ambiguous. The floating charge actually contained not one but *two* negative pledge clauses. The first was a negative pledge of the sort described above, namely one conferring priority in ranking on the floating charge as against any subsequent standard security or other ordinary security. The second was a blanket prohibition of any sort of security at all—even a postponed security.[1] Were Bass merely waiving the first clause? Or both? When the company went into receivership, this ambiguity was litigated, and in 1998 Lord Cameron of Lochbroom held that the consent to the security did not disturb the prior ranking of the floating charge.[2]

The Bank of Ireland responded to that decision by making an application for judicial rectification of the letter of consent under s 8 of the Law Reform (Miscellaneous Provisions) (Scotland) Act 1985.[3] But Bass argued that rectification could make no difference. Section 464(1A) of the Companies Act 1985 states that the effect of a negative pledge clause is to confer priority on the floating charge. To disapply that, argued Bass, a mere letter of consent, however worded, would be insufficient. What would be required would be a duly registered instrument of alteration in terms of s 466. Lord Macfadyen held that it would, and that a registered instrument of alteration was not necessary in order to disapply s 464(1)(A).

Rather curiously, no reference was made to *Scottish & Newcastle plc v Ascot Inns Ltd*.[4] In that case the creditor in a floating charge wrote to the debtor company releasing 21 heritable properties from the ambit of the floating charge. But nothing was registered in terms of s 466. The floating charge later attached and the creditor claimed that the charge extended to the whole property of the company, including the 21 properties in question. It was held that the letter had effectually released those properties. Although the two cases are not precisely the same, the essential issues are very similar.

---

1 Such clauses are not uncommon. To what extent they are actually enforceable is a complex question. As against the debtor they are contractually valid. But damages are pointless against an insolvent debtor, while if the debtor is solvent no loss will arise to the lender anyway. In rare cases interdict may be possible. Whether reduction is available depends on whether the clause is valid against third parties. No one really knows the answer to that question, and there are arguments both ways. One obvious problem for the lender—and this is relevant whether enforcement is sought against the debtor or a third party—is that it is difficult to see why a postponed security should prejudice the rights of the first lender anyway. Indeed, that line of thought makes one wonder why such clauses are inserted in the first place. These issues are too large to be entered into here.

2 *Griffith and Powdrill (Receivers of Lewis Lloyd Holdings Ltd) Petrs* 1998 GWD 40–2037.

3 The decision in so far as it relates to rectification is discussed again below at pp 118–119.

4 1994 SLT 1140.

It might be worth observing that both decisions may create problems for third parties, and in particular for a person purchasing from a receiver. The third party purchaser may, on the basis of the contents of the Companies Register, think that the charge has priority over a subsequent standard security, or that the particular property being purchased has not been released from the charge and is therefore subject to sale by the receiver. But both beliefs may turn out to be false on the basis of unregistered documentation contradicting registered documentation. Thus, the decision in *Bank of Ireland* v *Bass Brewers*, though reasonable as between the parties, may turn out to be unsatisfactory in the wider context.

It is perhaps therefore worth observing that there exists a difference between ranking agreements with personal effect and ranking agreements with real effect. The latter actually change the ranking. A liquidator, for example, must respect the terms of the ranking agreement and write the cheques accordingly. But a ranking agreement with personal effect has effect only as between the two creditors involved. In such a case a liquidator will ignore the agreement. Having received their cheques, so to speak, the parties must make a mutual adjustment in accordance with their agreement. It might be argued that in the present case the agreement, not having been registered, had personal but not real effect.

The CML Handbook

The Council of Mortgage Lenders (CML) published *The CML Lenders Handbook for Scotland* (also available at www.cml.org.uk). Part 1 contains rules applicable to all mortgages with CLM member institutions. Part 2 gives rules for particular lending institutions. The idea is that the rules will have contractual effect by being referred to in the instructions to the solicitor. Much of Part 1 is commonsensical and does little more than formulate what was always recognised as good practice anyway. But there may be cause for concern about the wording of some of the provisions, especially given the increasing readiness of lenders who fail to recover their money from their customers to pursue claims against law firms, claims which, in certain cases, seem to amount to no more than an unfair attempt to shift to the law firm responsibility for a bad lending decision, a responsibility which presumptively should rest with the professional moneylender who made it in the first place.

Conveyancers will have to familiarise themselves with this booklet, since non-compliance will open the door to claims, plus the loss of panel status.

Paragraph 3.3 requires the solicitor to check the identity of the signatory of the security. That is of course proper professional practice in any case, but it lays down how the check is to be done. Roughly speaking, the solicitor must see either (a) the passport or (b) *two* out of a list of items such as credit cards and council tax bills (not more than three months old). The apparent validity of the item must be checked and photocopies kept on file. The solicitor must check that 'the address shown on any document used to verify identity is that of the signatory'. S/he must also check that 'the signatory's signature on any document being used to verify identity matches the signatory's signature' on the standard security.

It seems that these requirements do not apply where the solicitor 'personally know[s] the signatory.' But the cautious conveyancer will be cautious about relying on that exemption.

Paragraph 4.1.1.1 states that the solicitor 'must take reasonable steps to verify that there are no discrepancies between the description of the property as valued and the title and other documents which a reasonably competent conveyancer should obtain'. The precise meaning of this provision is perhaps not perfectly clear. It may mean that when drafting the missives, and also when examining title, the survey report must be checked.

Paragraph 5.1.1 says that 'if the proprietor has owned the property for less than six months' the lender must be informed. The meaning of this provision is rather puzzling, but from the context it seems to be directed mainly at the case where the borrowing client is purchasing from a seller who has owned the property for less than six months, so that 'proprietor' effectively means 'seller'. Whether the provision covers other cases such as remortgages is unclear.

Paragraph 5.1.2 contains a provision which is important because of its generality:

> If any matter comes to the attention of the fee earner dealing with the transaction which you should reasonably expect us to consider important in deciding whether or not to lend to the borrower (such as whether the borrower has given misleading information to us or the information which you might reasonably expect to have been given to us is no longer true) and you are unable to disclose that information to us because of a conflict of interest, you must cease to act for us . . .

Curiously, this does not say that the information should be revealed where there is no conflict of interest. Perhaps such an obligation may be implied. The distinction between 'you' and the 'fee earner' is presumably a deliberate one, but its significance is unclear. Leaving such points on one side, this paragraph is *multum in parvo* and may prove to be the most important, and, to the solicitor, most worrying, in the Handbook.

Paragraph 5.4.1: 'The title to the property must be good and marketable, free of any burdens, restrictions, servitudes, charges or encumbrances which, at the time of settlement, might reasonably be expected to materially adversely affect the value of the property or its future marketability . . .'[1] The wording is strong. Suppose that there is a real burden forbidding any 'trade business or profession'. Probably a majority of dwellinghouses have some such burden. Unless one can be sure that planning permission would never be granted for commercial use, such a burden is likely to lessen the value of the property, for a property which is available for both residential and commercial use must, other things being equal, be worth more than a property which is limited to just one use. Hence, a solicitor who does not specially report on such a burden to the lender may be in breach of 5.4.1. But this can hardly be what is intended.

---

1 This sentence contains one of the most remarkable split infinitives in the history of the language.

Paragraph 5.8 states that the lender requires that in a purchase the client provides the whole balance of the price 'from his own funds' and the solicitor must check that this is so.

Paragraph 5.10.3 says that

> if you are aware that any transfer of the title to the property may be open to challenge as a gratuitous alienation or unfair preference, then you must be satisfied that we will acquire our interest in good faith and will be protected under the relevant statutory provisions ... You must also obtain clear personal searches against all parties to any such transfer. If you are unable to give an unqualified certificate of title you must arrange indemnity insurance.

This will provide further impetus for the change in conveyancing practice which began some years ago. The reference to protection 'under the relevant statutory provisions' is perhaps inadequate from the standpoint of the lender since gratuitous alienations and unfair preferences can be reduced under the common law rules as well as the statutory ones, and the defences to a common law action are themselves common law defences and not statutory ones.

No one really knows what one must do to ensure the status of being in good faith. Indeed, what amounts to good faith is arguably a moving target, in that it may change as standards of good conveyancing practice change. It may be that what is required is not only a clear personal search, but also, in appropriate cases, an affidavit of solvency from the granter of the gratuitous conveyance.

For instance, if Jack dispones gratuitously to Jill, and Jill grants a standard security to a bank, then it is probably advisable (from the standpoint of the law agents for the bank) to obtain an affidavit of solvency from Jack.[1] If that is obtained, and if there is a clear personal search against Jack, that is probably enough. It should be recalled that a gratuitous alienation can be challenged for as long as five years after the alienation.[2] Indeed, under the common law rules there is no specific time limit at all. Despite the common law rules, current conveyancing practice considers that if the gratuitous alienation took place over five years ago, and there exists a clear personal search against the granter for five years after the alienation, that is sufficient to establish good faith. Thus, if Jack dispones to Jill in year 1, and it is now year 8, a clear search against Jack for five years after the disposition will show that he was not sequestrated in that period, and that therefore the possibility of a challenge is minimal.[3] Forms 10—13 for the Land Register provide for a personal search for only five years *back from the certificate*. This in theory might be regarded as inadequate. Thus, suppose that Jack dispones to Jill in year 1 and is sequestrated in year 2. In year 8 Jill proposes to grant a standard security to a bank. A search against Jack for five

---

1 This may be necessary *anyway*, according to current good-practice standards, whether or not a security is being granted.

2 Bankruptcy (Scotland) Act 1985, s 34; Insolvency Act 1986, s 242. If the transferee is unconnected with the granter the period is only two years.

3 In theory a challenge can be made outwith the context of sequestration (or liquidation) but in practice this is rare, and moreover any action of reduction will normally be accompanied by a Notice of Summons of Reduction registered in the Personal Register.

years backwards will not reveal the sequestration. The risk is small, but the best practice is to search the Personal Register against the granter for five years following the deed in question.

In Sasine transactions (including first registrations) the same may also apply in relation to *prior* parties. Thus, if Jack dispones gratuitously to Jill, and Jill sells to Fiona, and Fiona wishes to grant a security to a bank, it may be necessary, when acting for the bank, to seek an affidavit of solvency from Jack, and also a clear personal search against him for five years after his divestiture. In Land Register cases no information will usually be available about prior transactions and the bank can take the land certificate at face value.

Paragraph 6.2 says, about boundaries, that 'wherever possible, these must be clearly defined by reference to a suitable plan or description'. This should not normally be a problem for Land Register properties, but for the dwindling number of GRS cases it may sometimes be a problem. It probably means that a description which is little more than a postal address will be insufficient.

The Handbook contains a statement that it was prepared 'in close consultation' with the Law Society of Scotland, and the Society is quoted as saying that it 'is pleased to have been consulted by the Council of Mortgage Lenders about the contents of the handbook and hopes that this will be of assistance to practitioners in Scotland'. Whether that amounts to an endorsement is unclear.

Lastly, it may be mentioned that the main cover photograph of the *CML Lenders Handbook for Scotland* is of a Dutch farmhouse.

Cautionary wives

The 1997 decision of the House of Lords in *Smith v Bank of Scotland*[1] was one of major importance, not least for conveyancers. This introduced into Scots law the English doctrine associated with *Barclays Bank v O'Brien*.[2] To state the *O'Brien/ Smith* doctrine[3] with any degree of precision would be difficult.[4] Roughly it is this. A creditor owes to a potential cautioner, or to the grantor of a security which has cautionary effect, a duty of good faith. If, therefore, there is any reason to suppose that the consent of the cautioner might be obtained by the principal obligant by unfair means (by misrepresentation, by force and fear, or by undue influence), the creditor must take reasonable steps to ensure that this does not happen. If such reasonable steps are taken, then, even if it later turns out that the consent was procured by unfair means, the cautioner will still be liable.[5] In

---

1 1997 SC (HL) 111.
2 [1994] 1 AC 180.
3 In yoking the names thus it must not be supposed that the English and Scottish doctrines are absolutely identical. It is clear from *Smith* itself that they are not, and this has been confirmed by later cases, such as *Royal Bank of Scotland plc v Clark* 2000 SLT (Sh Ct) 101. However, the two doctrines are so similar, especially in terms of practical outcomes, that for many purposes they can be considered as one.
4 For an extended examination of the doctrine, see G L Gretton, 'Sexually Transmitted Debt' 1999 *Tydskrif vir die Suid-Afrikaanse Reg* 419. For a modern (English) account see G Andrews and R Millett, *Law of Guarantees* (3rd edn, 2000).
5 In such a case the cautioner is likely to have a claim against the principal obligant on account of the misrepresentation etc.

practice, the cautioners are usually wives, the loans in question having been made to their husbands' businesses. Hence, in England they are commonly called 'surety wives'. A kilt turns this into 'cautionary wives'. But of course the protection is, at least in theory, gender-neutral.

In England, where the doctrine has existed for some time—even before the landmark case of *O'Brien*—there has been a seemingly never-ending stream of case law. That the same would happen here, once the *O'Brien* doctrine was introduced, was almost inevitable. 2000 produced several such cases. As in England, so in Scotland, some rather weak cases are being fought out under the banner of the doctrine. The reason is plain. The cautionary wife is fighting in the last trench. She has nothing left to lose, and any half-stateable argument will be used. In practice, she often has the evidential support of the husband or other person who, she says, wrongfully induced her to sign. It may seem surprising that such a person will be happy to admit his own wrong. But since he is, in the usual case, bankrupt anyway, he has little to lose, and the family as a whole has much to gain.

One of the themes in recent litigation is whether the fact that the cautionary wife was advised by a solicitor is sufficient to protect the bank's good faith, even if the solicitor was also acting for the main debtor. Following English authority the courts have been answering that question in the affirmative.

In *Broadway* v *Clydesdale Bank plc*[1] Isabella Broadway and her husband, Leslie, and son Anthony, were co-owners of Westquarter House, Glassford, Strathaven, the shares being 25%, 25% and 50% respectively. They all lived in the house, together with Anthony's wife Sandra. There was a family company called Gardiner Environment Services Limited in which all four seem to have been involved. In 1992 Anthony and Sandra borrowed £200,000 from the Clydesdale Bank, apparently for the purpose of lending the money to the company. A standard security over the property was signed by all four. Isabella and Leslie did not become personally liable as cautioners for the loan, but, rather, granted security over their shares without incurring any personal liability. Though not cautioners in formal terms, they were in a position similar to that of cautioners.

Eventually there was default and the bank sought to enforce the security. Isabella raised the present action to reduce the security. She had, she said, signed as a result of the undue influence of her son. She had not received any advice before signing. The bank, she said, had not explained to her the meaning and effect of the deed and had not advised her to take legal advice. The defenders averred that she had been advised by her own solicitor, which she denied. The argument of the bank was that even if it was true that she had not received legal advice (and they did not concede that this was so), nevertheless they had reasonably believed that she had had the benefit of such advice, and that that was all that was necessary to establish that they had acted in good faith.

That is a correct statement of the law: what is in issue in cases of this sort is the good faith of the lender, and that is to a substantial extent a question of

---

1 2000 GWD 19–763.

how matters *appeared* to the lender at the relevant time rather than how things actually were at the relevant time. Nevertheless, the Lord Ordinary, in a careful and valuable opinion, declined to dismiss the action and allowed a proof before answer:

> A lender faced with unclear information as to whether or not a cautioner (the validity of whose consent to the security transaction may, because of a personal relationship between the borrower and the cautioner of which he is aware, be undermined) has the benefit of independent legal advice may, in order to preserve his good faith, be obliged to make inquiry seeking clarification of that point.

This seems a fair approach.

One of the key documents in the case was a letter from solicitors who, according to the bank, were acting for each member of the family, including Isabella, and this letter was addressed to 'the Broadway Family' and opened with the words 'Dear All'. Letters in such terms are perfectly understandable and indeed often represent good practice. Formality can put clients off. A family often acts as an entity. The family decides this or that. But it is evident that there is also a danger. Although the social and psychological reality may be that the family is acting as a unit, in law each member is a separate person, and thus, if a client at all, a separate client.[1] Instructions must be received from each and every person, and evidence of that preserved on file. When advice is given, it is important to ensure that it reaches all those whom it is supposed to reach.[2] Hence the dangers of writing a letter to, say, 'Mr and Mrs X', a letter which might easily be read by the one and not the other.

In *Royal Bank of Scotland plc v Clark*[3] Mrs Clark executed a standard security in favour of the Royal Bank of Scotland in respect of a loan to her husband's business. When the bank sought to enforce, she claimed that she had been induced to sign by her husband by force and fear. The bank averred that she had been advised at the time by a solicitor who acted both for her and for her husband. She denied this and averred that she had not been advised at all, but she seems also to have argued that, esto she had been advised, the fact that the solicitor was her husband's solicitor meant that the standards required by the *O'Brien/Smith* doctrine had not been met. Proof was allowed on the question of what advice she had received. But it was held that if she had been advised by her husband's solicitor, that was sufficient to protect the heritable creditor's good faith. Although the sheriff[4] observed that it would be wrong to assume that in this area Scots law is the same as English law, nevertheless he considered that in Scotland as in England it was reasonable for a lender to assume that a person who had been advised by a solicitor was giving a true and informed consent.

---

1 In saying this we are speaking generally and not prejudging the factual dispute in *Broadway* as to whether Isabella was or was not in fact a client.
2 Once again we are speaking generally and not prejudging the question of whether Isabella did or did not receive and read the letter in question. Nor are we suggesting that the solicitors were negligent in any way.
3 2000 SLT (Sh Ct) 101, 2000 SCLR 193.
4 Michael Fletcher, Dumfries.

One wonders, however, whether there is not another dimension to this case. Whereas misrepresentation and undue influence result in voidability, force and fear is generally regarded as resulting in absolute nullity. If in this case force and fear were to be proved, then the consequence, it is suggested, would be that the security would be, as far as the wife's interests were concerned, void, and that would be so whether or not the lender had been in good faith. Subject to certain particular exceptions, good faith does not protect against absolute nullity.[1]

In *Wright* v *Cotias Investments Inc*[2] Irene Wright was the owner of 3 Royal Terrace, Edinburgh. She had debts of £155,000 secured on the property. She set up a company called Bond Corporation Ltd, of which she was a director and (it seems) majority shareholder, and she granted to it a 25-year lease. This company borrowed £200,000 from Cotias. Wright granted a guarantee and also a standard security over her property. Wright paid off the existing loans with this money. How the £200,000 passed from the company to her to enable her to do this is obscure, as are many other factual aspects of the case. When Cotias sought to enforce the guarantee and standard security Wright raised an action of reduction and interdict. The basis was that her consent had not been free and informed. She alleged bad faith and fraud against a number of parties including one of her sons who, it seems, had been behind the whole arrangement. The action was dismissed as irrelevant. Although it is difficult to comment on the case because of the lack of clarity as to many factual issues, it appears that the dismissal was almost inevitable.

In *Royal Bank of Scotland plc* v *Wilson*[3] two brothers were partners. They and their wives granted standard securities to the Royal Bank of Scotland. The debts stated to be secured included the business debts of any party, and after the securities were granted such debts were incurred. The wives resisted enforcement on the ground that the bank should have informed them specifically of what was happening and, not having done so, was in bad faith. It was held that the defence was irrelevant, given that the wives had received legal advice when executing the securities. There seem to have been no averments that the husbands had been guilty of misrepresentation or other undue pressure.

In *Ahmed* v *Clydesdale Bank plc*[4] Kishwer Ahmed and her husband Riaz Ahmed bought flat G/R, 1735 Great Western Road, Glasgow in 1991. The purchase was financed by a loan from the Clydesdale Bank, secured by a standard security. The security deed bound each for the debts, present or future, owed by either to the bank.[5] Later Mr Ahmed wished to borrow further money from the bank,

---

1 *cf Harrison* v *Butters* 1969 SLT 183.
2 2000 SCLR 324, 2001 SLT 353.
3 2001 SLT (Sh Ct) 2.
4 2001 SLT 423.
5 The wording was typical of such deeds: '. . . to pay . . . all sums which are now and which may at any time hereafter become due to the Bank in any manner of way by . . . us, either solely or jointly with any person or persons or corporation, company, firm or other body, and whether as principal or surety.' There was a further declaration, again in typical style, that 'in the event of the personal obligation contained in this standard security being granted by more than one person, the said sums shall include all sums for which any one or more of the granters may now be or become liable to the Bank'.

and the bank wrote to Mrs Ahmed asking her to sign a guarantee. She refused to do so. Nevertheless, the loan went ahead. Mrs Ahmed was thus liable for this additional loan even though she had expressly declined to be liable for it. She raised an action to reduce the standard security over her half share in the property.

She did not plead that her husband had induced her to sign anything by way of misrepresentation or force and fear or undue influence. Her argument was that the bank had acted in bad faith in lending the money to Mr Ahmed in the knowledge that she did not wish to be liable therefor. Her action of reduction failed. Apart from any other consideration, Mrs Ahmed had had the benefit of legal advice when she signed the standard security.

It is indeed difficult to see why the standard security could be regarded as reducible because of a loan made later. As the Lord Ordinary (Macfadyen) observed, 'it was not argued on the pursuer's behalf that there were any circumstances adversely affecting the validity of the standard security when it was granted'. If Mrs Ahmed had a case, it was that she was not liable for the new loan. Since no objection was made to the standard security itself it is difficult to see on what grounds its reduction could be demanded. To quote Lord Macfadyen again:

> The obligation which the pursuer seeks to set aside, namely the standard security, was entered into by her, in circumstances which are not impugned, long before the alleged acts of bad faith. If the allegedly misleading letter had never been sent, the pursuer's position would have been no different from her present position.

One might wonder why the pursuer sought to have the standard security reduced even in respect of the original home loan. Whilst we have not had the benefit of seeing the written pleadings, the opinion of the Lord Ordinary indicates that that was part of the conclusions of the summons.

The core of Mrs Ahmed's case was that she should not have been liable for the further loan. If that could have been established, then it would follow that her half share of the property would not be affected by the loan. In fact her case was a strong one. A standard security in the form which she signed works as a mutual cautionary obligation, and for future as well as existing indebtedness. But it is a principle of the law of cautionary obligations that if caution is granted for future advances to the principal obligant, the cautioner is free at any time, by notice, to withdraw, with the result that if the creditor chooses to make further advances to the principal obligant, those advances will not be secured by the cautionary obligation. (Naturally, termination does not free the cautioner from liability for *existing* debt.) Now, when Mrs Ahmed intimated her refusal to grant the guarantee, that can readily be construed as a withdrawal of her cautionary liability for future borrowings by the principal obligant from the creditor.[1] On this analysis she would have had no liability for the new loan, nor would her half-share have been affected by it.

---

1 In an arrangement of this sort each party is in fact both cautioner and principal obligant. But for present purposes the focus is on the husband as principal obligant.

All these cases were fought out between the lender and the cautionary wife. But there is another side to the story. If the cautionary wife loses—and the trend of recent case law on both sides of the border is that the cautionary wife usually does lose[1]—then she may have a claim against the solicitor who advised her. Every action of reduction by a cautionary wife which fails because she was advised by a solicitor is a potential negligence claim against a law firm. That is not to say that such a claim will have merit, or be successful.[2] But it cannot be emphasised enough that advising a cautionary wife is fraught with danger.[3]

The Mortgage Rights (Scotland) Bill

This Member's Bill[4]—as to whose anglicising title we will here express no opinion—is currently being considered by the Scottish Parliament. It was introduced by Cathie Craigie on 3 July 2000 and completed stage 1 of the Bill procedure on 17 January 2001. It seems to have the Executive's support, and so it may well be passed. It aims to confer on the courts a discretion to suspend the rights of heritable creditors in residential mortgages. The key provisions (as of January 2001) are as follows:

1 Application to suspend enforcement of standard security

(1) This section applies where a creditor in a standard security over an interest in land has

   (a) served (i) a calling-up notice under s 19 (calling-up of standard security), or (ii) a notice of default under s 21 (notice of default), of the Conveyancing and Feudal Reform (Scotland) Act 1970 . . .

   (b) made an application to the court under s 24 (application to court for remedies on default) of that Act, or

   (c) commenced proceedings under s 5 (power to eject proprietor in personal occupancy) of the Heritable Securities (Scotland) Act 1894 . . .

(2) The following persons may apply to the court for an order under s 2 of this Act—

   (a) the debtor in the standard security or the proprietor of the security subjects (where the proprietor is not the debtor), if the security subjects (in whole or in part) are that person's sole or main residence,

   (b) the non-entitled spouse of the debtor or the proprietor, where the security subjects (in whole or in part) are a matrimonial home and the sole or main residence of the non-entitled spouse but not of the debtor or, as the case may be, the proprietor.

---

1 This may be because banks are settling cases where there are real merits in the cautionary wife's case.
2 Which are not the same concepts.
3 See G L Gretton, 'Good News for Bankers—Bad News for Lawyers?' 1999 SLT (News) 53.
4 'Member's bill' is the name given in Holyrood to what in Westminster would be called a 'private member's bill'.

(3) An application under subsection (2) must be made—

    (a) in the case mentioned in subsection (1)(a)(i), before the expiry of the period of notice specified in the calling-up notice,

    (b) in the case mentioned in subsection (1)(a)(ii), not later than one month after the expiry of the period of notice specified in the notice of default,

    (c) in a case mentioned in subsection (1)(b) or (c), before the conclusion of the proceedings.

(4) An application under subsection (2) in a case mentioned in subsection (1)(a) must be made by summary application.

2 Disposal of application

(1) On an application under s 1(2) the court may—

    (a) suspend the exercise of the rights which the creditor has, or may acquire, by virtue of the enactments mentioned in subsection (1)(a) to (c) of that section (i) to such extent, (ii) for such period, and (iii) subject to such conditions, as the court thinks fit,

    (b) if the application is made in proceedings under s 24 of the Conveyancing and Feudal Reform (Scotland) Act 1970 or s 5 of the Heritable Securities (Scotland) Act 1894, continue those proceedings to such date as the court thinks fit.

(2) The court may make an order under this section only where it considers it reasonable in all the circumstances to do so; and the court, in considering whether to make such an order and what its terms should be, is to have regard in particular to—

    (a) the nature of and reasons for the default,

    (b) the applicant's ability to fulfil within a reasonable period the obligations under the standard security in respect of which the debtor is in default, and

    (c) the ability of the applicant and any other person residing at the security subjects to secure reasonable alternative accommodation.

(3) If, while an order under this section is in force, the obligations under the standard security in respect of which the debtor is in default are fulfilled, the standard security has effect as if the default had not occurred.

The Mortgage Rights (Scotland) Bill has attracted both support and opposition, the latter coming, for example, from the Council for Mortgage Lenders.[1] Whether the Bill, if enacted, would make any dramatic difference may perhaps be doubted. It is difficult to see the judiciary destroying the mortgage system as we know it by refusing to give effect to standard securities. One suspects that suspensions will in practice be in terms of months rather than years. Those lenders with socially responsible enforcement policies no doubt have the least to fear.

---

1 For evidence submitted to the Social Inclusion Committee of the Scottish Parliament not only by the CML but by other organisations, such as the Law Society, COSLA, Scottish Homes, Shelter Scotland, Citizens Advice Scotland, see www.scottish.parliament.uk/official_report/cttee/social-00/sor00–04–04.htm#anb05

PASSING OF PROPERTY

From receivership to sequestration

In *Sharp v Thomson*[1] it was held by the House of Lords, reversing the Court of Session, that purchasers who had taken delivery of a disposition were protected against the receivership of the sellers. This protection operated even although the disposition had not been registered. What was the *ratio* of the decision? No one is quite sure, but one view—admittedly based more on Lord Jauncey's speech than Lord Clyde's—is that on delivery of the deed[2] the sellers were divested of any 'beneficial interest' in the property (a flat). No doubt they remained owners in some narrow sense. Only registration of the purchasers could remove this 'ownership' from the sellers. But that ownership was an empty shell. The flat was held for the purchasers. In those circumstances it would be wrong to treat the flat as still within the 'property and undertaking' of the sellers, within the meaning of s 462(1) of the Companies Act 1985. Hence, as a matter of statutory interpretation, when the floating charge previously granted by the sellers attached prior to registration of the disposition, the flat escaped the floating charge and passed unencumbered to the purchasers.

So potentially radical were the changes effected by *Sharp* that much remained—and remains—unclear. An obvious issue was whether the new rule applied to all insolvency processes or whether it was confined to receivership alone. On this question, the two judges to give speeches (Lords Jauncey and Clyde) did not seem at one. For Lord Jauncey it was self-evident that the rule would apply to other insolvency processes as well. Indeed, his speech seems to presuppose that that was *already* the law. But Lord Clyde appeared to take the opposite view, stressing that the decision turned on an interpretation of the legislation on floating charges, and indicating that a delivered disposition would not prevail against an adjudication against the seller.[3] The law was thus left unclear. A broad interpretation of *Sharp* would extend the rule to sequestration and liquidation; a narrow view would confine it to receivership. The choice remained to be made.

In *Burnett's Tr v Grainger*[4] the choice had to be made. In October 1990 Mr and Mrs Grainger concluded missives to buy 94 Malcolm Road, Peterculter, from Mrs Burnett. The transaction settled on 8 November 1990, when the disposition was delivered in exchange for payment of the price. The disposition was not recorded until 27 January 1992, some 14 months later. But in the meantime Mrs

---

1 1997 SC(HL) 66, 1997 SLT 636, 1997 SCLR 328.

2 And payment, though how relevant this was to the decision is unclear.

3 The significance of this point is that sequestration is a deemed adjudication: see Bankruptcy (Scotland) Act 1985, s 31(1)(b).

4 2000 SLT (Sh Ct) 116. For commentary on this case, see R Rennie, 'To *Sharp v Thomson*—an Heir' 2000 SLT (News) 247; S C Styles, '*Sharp* Pains for Scots Property Law: The Case of *Burnett's Tr v Grainger*' 2000 SLT (News) 305; G L Gretton, 'Equitable Ownership in Scots Law?' (2001) 5 *Edinburgh Law Review* 73.

Burnett had been sequestrated, and on 10 December 1991 her trustee completed title to the house by recording a notice of title.

Before *Sharp* the law was fairly clear: events of the kind just described would be analysed as involving what has long been known as a 'race to the register'. There would be two competitors: Mr and Mrs Grainger, on the one hand, and, on the other, the trustee in sequestration. As is usual in races, the first to get to the finishing line wins. Since it was the trustee who won the race, the property would go to him, and not to the Graingers. That would be painful for them, but they would have had no one to blame but themselves.[1]

But on a broad interpretation of *Sharp* the analysis would be different. Purely by delivery of the disposition Mrs Burnett would be divested of any 'beneficial interest' in the house, which would cease to form part of the 'whole estate of the debtor' within s 31(1) of the Bankruptcy (Scotland) Act 1985. Although the trustee had registered and the purchasers had not, the house would go to the purchasers. The trustee had reached the finishing line first, but the race would be called off.

The arguments in *Burnett's Tr* were along predictable lines. The trustee argued that *Sharp* should be narrowly interpreted, and the case decided on the traditional basis of a race to the register. The purchasers urged the court to follow Lord Jauncey and extend the doctrine of *Sharp* to sequestration. The purchasers were successful. The sheriff principal (D J Risk QC) found consistency in the speeches of Lords Jauncey and Clyde, and concluded that the rule in *Sharp* was not confined to receivership. Accordingly, once the disposition had been delivered and the price paid, the purchasers were safe from the seller's insolvency.

The decision has been appealed, but whether the appeal will in fact go ahead is at present uncertain.

Six objections

The decision in *Sharp* attracted a large literature, most of it hostile.[2] The numerous articles and commentaries may be summarised as offering six main objections to *Sharp*—and now, by extension, to *Burnett's Tr* as well.[3]

First, the cases are a solution to a non-problem. A conveyancing transaction settles on the basis of an interim report in the property and personal registers. If the seller is a company there is also a search in the register of charges and a letter of non-crystallisation from the holder of any floating charge. Since the registers are more or less up-to-date, the searches are up-to-date in turn. Thus a purchaser knows, before paying, whether there is a danger of insolvency. Naturally, the information flow is not perfect. There is a blind period beginning with the date of the interim report and ending with the date of registration of the disposition. If the seller is sequestrated during this period, or if a floating charge crystallises, the purchaser is at risk. But the period is short, usually not

---

1 Or their solicitors. As to whether there was in fact negligence in this case we have no information.
2 The main articles are listed at para 11.31 note 6 of G L Gretton and K G C Reid, *Conveyancing* (2nd edn, 1999).
3 What follows is the merest sketch of a subject of considerable complexity.

more than a few days. And even for this brief period the purchaser is protected—by the letter of obligation granted by the seller's solicitor (and backed by insurance), and, if there are floating charges, by a letter of non-crystallisation by the charge holder. The purchaser who registers with normal expedition has nothing to fear.

In neither of the two cases did the purchaser register promptly. The interval between settlement and registration was 15 months in *Sharp* and 14 months in *Burnett's Tr*. In both cases prompt registration would have avoided any problem. Normally a delay on this scale would be professional negligence on the part of the solicitors concerned, although we offer no views on the particular facts of those cases.[1] The decision in *Sharp* was an attempt to remedy what was seen as an injustice intrinsic to the Scottish system of land transfer: the buyer paid the money and received nothing in return. But far from being intrinsic to the system, the injustice (if such it is) occurs only where normal conveyancing procedures are not followed.

The second objection is that *Sharp* and *Burnett's Tr* offer only half a solution. If there is a problem, then it is not properly solved by these decisions. Purchasers are protected against insolvency processes occurring *after* delivery of the disposition. They are not protected by those occurring *before*. This means that not all of the blind period is covered. Suppose for example that a floating charge attaches, with the appointment of a receiver, at 11.31 am on the morning of settlement.[2] If the transaction settled at 11.29 am, the purchaser takes the property free of the floating charge. But if it settled at 11.33 am the floating charge strikes.

Third, in (half) solving one (non) problem, the cases create another problem which is more serious, and less easily managed. Following the decisions in *Sharp* and, now, in *Burnett's Tr*, no one can safely take a title from a receiver, a trustee in sequestration or, probably, a liquidator. This problem is discussed further below.

Fourth, the decisions leave the law uncertain in many respects. Whether the rule in *Sharp* extends to sequestration depends on the result of a possible appeal in *Burnett's Tr*. If sequestration is included, then so, probably, is liquidation. The position of adjudication, however, would remain uncertain. And there are other uncertainties. Does the rule protect donees as well as purchasers? Does it apply to judicial transfers, and to transfers effected by statute? Is the rule confined to land or does it apply also to incorporeal property such as shares? Does it apply to deeds other than dispositions, such as leases and standard securities?[3]

Fifth, the decisions violate the principle that rights in land cannot be created without publicity.[4] This 'principle of publicity', as it tends to be called elsewhere,[5] is in Scotland often called the principle of the faith of the registers. Rights in

---

1 There may, for example, be other factors of which we are unaware.
2 The appointment of a receiver takes effect on the day and at the time when the instrument of appointment is delivered to the receiver: see Insolvency Act 1986, s 53(6)(b).
3 It may apply to standard securities: see *Halifax plc* v *Gorman's Tr* 2000 SLT 1409, discussed below.
4 See, eg K G C Reid, *The Law of Property in Scotland* (1996); D J Kleyn and A Boraine, *Silberberg & Schoeman's Law of Property* (3rd edn, 1992) pp 63–66.
5 German lawyers inevitably make it one word: *die Publizitätsprinzip*.

land should appear on the register or, if that is impossible, should be vouched by some public act, in practice usually possession. A real right of lease, for example, can be created either by registration or by possession. The introduction of registration of title marks a further move towards the primacy of registration. Its value would be substantially defeated if significant rights could be created without publicity. Yet that is what *Sharp* proposes. 'Beneficial interest' is lost, and gained, merely by delivery of a deed—a private act known only to the granter and grantee concerned. That would be acceptable if delivery affected only those parties, but that is not the position. The loss of 'beneficial interest' affects the receiver, or trustee in sequestration, or liquidator of the granter; and so it affects anyone transacting with those parties in relation to that property.

Indeed, the effect of *Sharp* and *Burnett's Tr* is to raise serious doubt as to whether registration has any real value to a purchaser. Why bother to register? What benefit is obtained thereby? More or less the only remaining reason to register is to protect the purchaser from a fraudulent second sale (or grant of a security) by the seller, though even here there are indications that the courts might hold the first purchaser to be protected. Is Scots law reverting to unregistered conveyancing? If so, the development is hardly to be welcomed.

Finally, the decisions damage the structure of our law by introducing the new,[1] and unexplained, concept of 'beneficial interest'. Beneficial interest may possibly be a disguised constructive trust; or an in-between right lying somewhere between personal rights and real rights. Or again it might be a sort of ownership, thus introducing the legal/beneficial duality found in English law. Of these only the first is even arguably compatible with Scots law, and then only barely so.[2] The others threaten the fundamentals on which our system of property law is built. If the distinction between real and personal rights is dismantled, we will have to create a new system of property law and conveyancing.

Practicalities

The decision in *Burnett's Tr* may not survive the appeal, if it proceeds. But if the decision is not reversed, and becomes accepted as good law, what would be the implications for everyday practice?

For standard transactions, it would mean that the purchaser would be unaffected by the sequestration of the seller once the transaction had been settled by delivery of the disposition. Thus, the 'blind period' would be restricted, in this respect at least, to the period between the interim report and settlement. If the seller were sequestrated after settlement but before registration of the disposition, this would have no effect on the title of the purchaser. This would mean that the trust clauses, introduced into dispositions following the earlier (and now reversed) judgments in *Sharp*, could be discarded, as in

---

1 Outside the field of trusts.
2 For the case against constructive trusts, see G L Gretton, 'Constructive Trusts' (1997) 1 *Edinburgh Law Review* 281 and 408.

practice has already substantially happened. Beyond this, no change in practice would be needed. In particular, the letter of obligation would continue to be required, partly because it covers more than sequestration, and partly because the purchaser is still at risk from sequestrations occurring *before* settlement.

For one particular type of transaction, however, *Burnett's Tr* would, if correct, have a major impact. The effect of *Sharp* was to cast doubt on the wisdom of taking title from a receiver. *Burnett's Tr* extends that doubt to trustees in sequestration and, probably, to liquidators as well.[1] The difficulty is caused by the breach of the publicity principle, mentioned earlier. Delivery of the disposition is not a public act. It cannot be discovered from a search of the registers. Thus, a person buying from a trustee in sequestration (or receiver or liquidator) cannot be sure that the bankrupt has not previously granted a disposition of the property. On the facts of *Burnett's Tr* a search of the register would have found only the trustee's notice of title; yet delivery of the disposition to the Graingers had taken the property out of the sequestration.

The risks here should not be exaggerated. Delivered but unregistered dispositions will probably be rare; and when they do occur they may be challengeable on some ground of insolvency law, such as gratuitous alienation. But bankrupts do not always behave honourably, and the decision in *Burnett's Tr* seems a positive invitation to grant unregistered dispositions. So while the risk is small, it is not so small as to be negligible. And if things do go wrong, the consequences are grave. If a disposition has indeed been delivered, the trustee (or receiver, or liquidator) has no title to sell. Hence, the purchaser would receive nothing. All of this may point towards title insurance, but much here depends on the attitude of the Keeper. Following *Sharp* the Keeper indicated that he would not normally exclude indemnity in purchases from a receiver, provided the purchaser's agent had made appropriate inquiries.[2] It is to be hoped that this approach will now be extended to include trustees in sequestration and liquidators.

One final point to note is that case law—unlike statute law—operates retrospectively. The rule asserted in *Burnett's Tr* is, if it is law at all, not merely law from 28 August 2000. It is deemed always to have been the law. For Sasine transactions and first registrations this extends the problem, noted above, back into the prescriptive period. If one of the deeds in the prescriptive progress was granted by a trustee in sequestration (or receiver or liquidator) there is the theoretical risk that the conveyance was inept due to an unregistered conveyance by the bankrupt.

---

1 The sheriff principal was unmoved by difficulties of this kind: 'if the ratio of *Sharp v Thomson* applies directly to this case, I am bound to follow it and, even if it does not apply precisely, if the reasoning of the House gives me clear guidance on the issue in this case, I would be well advised to follow it, *whatever the practical consequences*' (p 124I) (emphasis added).

2 See 1997 *Journal of the Law Society of Scotland* 507. Whether this would defeat the grantee of the delivered disposition is unclear, however. Certainly the purchaser would become owner, on registration in the Land Register; but the grantee might seek an order that the purchaser must convey to him, on the basis of *Short's Tr v Chung (No 2)* 1999 SLT 751.

INSOLVENCY

Securities granted by undischarged bankrupts

Can an undischarged bankrupt grant a valid standard security? It might be supposed that the question never arises in practice. After all, who would take security without a personal search against the debtor? And who, on seeing the search, would be prepared to proceed? Yet, precisely this state of affairs does sometimes arise.

If the property in question formed part of the estate at the time of sequestration, then it is clear that the security is invalid. There are two reasons for this, for the legislation takes a belt-and-braces approach. The first is that as soon as a sequestration petition is lodged an entry is made in the Register of Inhibitions and Adjudications, and that entry has the effect of an inhibition.[1] The second is that s 32(8) of the Bankruptcy (Scotland) Act 1985 says that (subject to certain exceptions) 'any dealing of or with the debtor relating to his estate . . . shall be of no effect in a question with the permanent trustee'. In an important 19th-century case, a borrower undertook to grant a heritable security over 95 acres. By some error the security as granted covered only five acres. After the debtor was sequestrated he granted a supplementary security over the remaining area. It was held that this was invalid.[2]

But what if the property in question was itself acquired after the sequestration? The typical example is where the bankrupt buys heritable property with the assistance of a loan and grants a standard security at the same time. Does it make any difference that this property is, by the nature of the case, not part of the estate as it existed at the opening of the proceedings?

Before addressing that question, it is worth asking why such securities are ever granted. There are three possibilities. The first is that, by reason of administrative error, no notice was ever registered in the Register of Inhibitions and Adjudications.[3] The second is that such a notice was registered but that for some reason the search failed to disclose it.[4] The third is that no search was done. Unfortunately, the reported cases seldom reveal the reasons.

If property is acquired by an undischarged bankrupt (*ie acquirenda* as opposed to *acquisata*), it vests in the trustee in sequestration.[5] But, curiously, neither of the two protections mentioned above seems to apply to such property. The notice registered in the Personal Register has the effect of an inhibition, but an inhibition

---

1 Bankruptcy (Scotland) Act 1985, s 14.
2 *Inglis* v *Mansfield (Stuart's Trustee)* (1835) 1 Shaw & Maclean 203. Under modern law the creditor might have been able to salvage his position by an application for rectification.
3 At least one firm of searchers, Messrs Miller & Bryce, offer a personal search which covers not only the Register of Inhibitions and Adjudications but also the Register of Insolvencies. Such a search is more reliable, since sometimes a sequestration is registered in the latter but not in the former. Moreover, the Register of Insolvencies contains more information about sequestrations than does the Register of Inhibitions and Adjudications.
4 This can happen for a variety of reasons. One is simple human error. Another is that there may be a mismatch between the search instructions and what is registered. The problem is precisely the same as for inhibitions.
5 1985 Act, s 32(6).

affects only property held at the time of the inhibition. It does not affect after-acquired property. So the deemed inhibition created by the registered notice probably does not affect property acquired by an undischarged bankrupt. Furthermore, the wording of s 32(8) of the Bankruptcy (Scotland) Act 1985, mentioned above, is limited to the estate as it existed at the opening of the sequestration. It does not apply to *acquirenda*.[1]

This does not mean that the trustee is powerless in relation to *acquirenda*. He can sell it or complete a title in his own name. But unless or until he does so, there is a danger that the bankrupt will grant a real right—perhaps a security or a disposition—to a third party, and it may be that such a deed cannot be attacked. The law is unclear.

Halifax plc v Gorman's Trustee[2] is the latest case on this problem. The petition for Jeanne Neil Gorman's sequestration was lodged on 15 October 1991 and sequestration was awarded on 9 January 1992. Sequestration is backdated to the lodging of the petition, so anything Gorman acquired after 15 October was *acquirenda*, even if acquired before 9 January. This is of course odd, for it means that assets acquired *before* the award of sequestration are *post-sequestration* assets.[3]

That is exactly what happened in the present case. Ms Gorman bought a property at 42 Russell Street, Johnstone, and the transaction settled on 31 December 1991, at which time the Halifax released the loan funds in exchange for a standard security.

Was there a search? If not, why not? If there was, did it disclose the sequestration petition? If not, why not? If it did disclose it, why did the Halifax proceed? We do not know the answers to these questions.

The feu disposition and standard security were presented to the Keeper. On Valentine's Day 1992 the Keeper registered Gorman as owner in the Land Register. But he refused to register the standard security, on the ground that it was a deed by an undischarged bankrupt which did not contain the consent of the trustee in sequestration.[4] Four years then passed, and on 25 June 1996 the trustee completed title to the property.

---

1 In *Halifax plc v Gorman's Tr* 2000 SLT 1409 (to be considered shortly) Lord Eassie (at 1417D–E) made the following valuable observation: 'Although not subject to any express mention by either counsel, I would add that subs (8) of s 32 of the 1985 Act expressly nullifies, in a question with the permanent trustee, dealings after sequestration by a bankrupt with the assets vesting, under s 31, in the trustee at the date of sequestration, but that provision is subject to various exceptions set out in subs (9). It appears to me that it would be at the least odd were certain dealings by a bankrupt with estate which had vested under s 31 to be protected by those exceptions, but any dealing whatever by the bankrupt with the subsequently acquired assets to be beyond any redemption by reason of the instantaneous, automatic and absolute vesting for which counsel for the defender contended.'

2 2000 SLT 1409.

3 1985 Act, s 12(4). The account given here has been simplified, but in substance is accurate.

4 A better course of action would surely have been to register the security but subject to exclusion of indemnity. The Lord Ordinary observed (at p 1418J) that 'neither counsel submitted that the Keeper was wrong to refuse registration'. Such an argument would not have been in the interests of the defender. The pursuers' case was that the standard security was effective even though unregistered, and so the Keeper's refusal did not at the end of the day make any real difference. One suspects that the pursuers, had they failed in this action, might perhaps have raised an action against the Keeper.

Eventually the Halifax raised an action for declarator that the (unregistered) standard security 'gives the pursuers, in competition with the defender, a prior right over those subjects (and the proceeds of any sale of them) to the extent of the sum owed by Mrs Gordon[1] to the pursuers'.

Since the standard security was unregistered one would suppose that it could be of no value to the Halifax. If the Halifax had a remedy, it was against the Keeper for his refusal to register the standard security. But in law, as in war, the outcome of battles is unpredictable. The Halifax won. They had two arguments.

The first was that s 32(6) of the Bankruptcy (Scotland) Act 1985—the sub-section which says that *acquirenda* vest in the trustee—is subject to a proviso: 'This subsection shall be without prejudice to any right or interest acquired in the estate in good faith and for value.' The defender conceded that the Halifax had acted in good faith.[2] The next question was therefore whether the Halifax had acquired a 'right or interest . . . in the estate'. The Lord Ordinary (Eassie) held that it had:[3] 'I do not consider it correct to say that prior to its being recorded a signed and delivered standard security is simply a piece of paper and cannot constitute at least an "interest" in the property over which it is granted.' With respect, that is not right. As Lord Rodger observed in another case from 2000, *Keeper of the Registers of Scotland v M R S Hamilton Ltd*:[4] 'If the proprietor grants a standard security over his registered interest, this has no effect on that interest unless or until it is registered.'[5] Of course, statute can do what it likes. Statute could declare a creditor's personal right fully effective against the debtor's trustee in sequestration. But to give an unregistered standard security the same effect as a registered one only the clearest statutory language would suffice. In fact the language of the proviso is vague and unspecific. But setting aside the details of the statutory language, there is a point of principle at stake here. *Sharp v Thomson*[6] and *Burnett's Tr v Grainger*[7] held that a disposition is effective without the need for registration. Now *Gorman* holds that a standard security is effective without registration. This is contrary to legal principle and to public policy. Whilst the facts in *Gorman* are certainly special facts, the wider implications are all too apparent.

The other argument for the Halifax was that Gorman had acquired the property by fraud and that it is a settled principle of law that a trustee in seques-tration cannot claim assets so acquired. No final decision on this argument was taken, but the Lord Ordinary said that, had he not decided the case on the first

---

1 Thus the name stands in both the SLT report and the text given on the Scottish Courts Service website.
2 It would be interesting to know why this was conceded. Had there been a clear search on which the Halifax had relied?
3 2000 SLT 1409 at 1417L.
4 2000 SLT 352 at 356.
5 And (though its specific facts were different) see the leading case of *Bank of Scotland v Hutchison Main & Co* 1913 SC 255, 1914 SC (HL) 1.
6 1997 SC (HL) 66, 1997 SLT 636, 1997 SCLR 328, discussed at pp 93–97 above.
7 2000 SLT (Sh Ct) 116, discussed above.

argument, he would have allowed a proof before answer on the second. In other words, he was not prepared to dismiss it as irrelevant. This approach seems open to question. The principle about fraud is true, but the property was not an asset acquired by fraud. There is no suggestion that the seller was defrauded, and even if that had happened the only result would have been that the seller could have demanded the return of the property. It may be that Ms Gorman did acquire an asset by fraud, but, if so, that asset was money, not land. There appears to be no rule that a claim for the return of money obtained by fraud has any special priority in a sequestration, and even if it did have such a priority that priority would not be attached to some other asset. This sort of 'tracing' is not admitted in Scots law. Indeed, the Bankruptcy (Scotland) Act 1985 has provision for such cases: the defrauded party is indeed protected, but in another way, the protection being the fact that the debtor's eventual discharge does *not* liberate her from the debt in question.[1]

There have been two previous reported cases on the problem: *Alliance & Leicester Building Society* v *Murray's Trustee*,[2] holding in favour of the trustee, and *Royal Bank of Scotland* v *Lamb's Trustee*,[3] holding in favour of the secured creditor. Curiously, the second case was not cited in *Gorman*. Nor did *Gorman* mention McBryde on *Bankruptcy*.[4]

Gorman was, it is respectfully suggested, not correctly decided, and it leaves open the difficult question as to which of *Murray's Trustee* and *Lamb's Trustee* was right. If *Lamb's Trustee* is right, the Keeper acted wrongly in rejecting the security.

One final thought. The conclusion sought was that the unregistered standard security 'gives the pursuers, in competition with the defender, a prior right over those subjects (and the proceeds of any sale of them) to the extent of the sum owed by Mrs Gordon [sic] to the pursuers'. One cannot help wondering how this was to be enforced. No problem would arise if the trustee were to sell. But if the trustee does not sell there would seem to be no way for the Halifax to realise its 'security'. If there was sufficient equity in the property then no doubt the trustee would sell, in which case the problem would be avoided.

Debtor discharged but heritable property still unrealised

What is the legal position if, by the time a debtor is discharged from his/her sequestration (which will normally be after three years), there is still some property left which has not been realised? That this should ever happen in practice may seem surprising, other than in the unusual case where assets come to light only at a late stage. But in fact it is not at all uncommon, even for assets

---

1 Section 55(2)(c).
2 1994 SCLR 19, 1995 SLT (Sh Ct) 77. The SCLR report cites the case as *Alliance & Leicester Building Society* v *Macgregor*.
3 1998 SCLR 923.
4 W W McBryde, *Bankruptcy* (2nd edn, 1995) para 9–163. This expresses the view that *Alliance & Leicester Building Society* v *Murray's Trustee* was rightly decided, though it should be observed that the work was published before *Lamb's Trustee*.

which are known to the trustee from the very beginning of the sequestration. It is a mystery, but a common one. When it happens, such assets do not revert to the debtor[1] but remain subject to the sequestration and the trustee retains the right—and indeed usually the duty—to realise them.

For heritable property, the legislation has a special provision to cover this case. Section 14(4) of the Bankruptcy (Scotland) Act 1985 says that the trustee may register a notice in the Register of Inhibitions and Adjudications before the expiry of the basic three-year period beginning with the sequestration itself. This renews for a further three years the inhibition achieved by registration of the original sequestration. The provision is a sensible one. The property stands in the name of a person who has been discharged from bankruptcy. To third parties it must appear that such property belongs to that person in the fullest sense. The effect of the registration in terms of s 14(4) is that third parties are alerted to the fact that all is not as it seems, and that whilst the debtor him/herself has been discharged, the sequestration itself is ongoing, and therefore that heritable property standing in the name of the ex-bankrupt may still be subject to the sequestration.

In *Roy's Trustee, Noter*[2] Ian Roy was sequestrated in 1992 and discharged three years later, in 1995. Some heritable property remained unrealised, but no notice under s 14(4) was registered. The Keeper's recommendation is that in such cases the trustee should seek judicial authority for late registration.[3] The court has a discretionary power, under s 63(1)(a) of the 1985 Act, to cure procedural defects. The sheriff (Alastair Stewart), however, refused the application as incompetent. Section 14(4) makes it quite clear that the notice must be registered before the expiry of the initial three-year period. To allow late registration would subvert the whole system, for third parties would no longer be able to rely on the Register of Inhibitions and Adjudications.

It has often been observed that cases, like buses, come in groups. The year 2000 saw another case on virtually the same facts, *Tewnion's Trustee, Noter*,[4] in which Sheriff David Kelbie came to exactly the same conclusion as Sheriff Stewart. There seems no doubt that the view of the law taken by the two sheriffs is correct.

Two footnotes may be added. The first is that in *Roy* the trustee seems to have argued that, unless the application were granted, third parties might be prejudiced, for they might act unaware that the property was still subject to the sequestration. That argument is unpersuasive. Section 44, as amended, of the Conveyancing (Scotland) Act 1924 has express provision for this situation. It says that where the notice has *not* been registered, third parties are protected.

The other footnote is that it must not be supposed that if late registration under s 14 is not possible then there is no solution. Although a notice under s 14(4) must be registered timeously, a trustee is free to complete title in his own

---

1 Unless they have been abandoned by the trustee, for which see below.
2 2000 SLT (Sh Ct) 77, 2000 SCLR 1105 (sub nom *Wright, Noter*).
3 At any rate that is what the trustee told the sheriff.
4 2000 SLT (Sh Ct) 37.

name (*qua* trustee in sequestration) *at any time*. For property in the Sasine Register this is done by recording a notice of title. For property in the Land Register such a notice is not necessary: the trustee simply applies for registration. It should be stressed that the fact that the debtor has been discharged does not prejudice this power to complete title.

It should be added that all this presupposes that the property in question has not been abandoned by the trustee, for if an asset is abandoned it falls out of the sequestration. The fact of the application to the sheriff shows that the trustee did not think that he had abandoned the property. But the sequestration happened in 1992, and it is difficult not to wonder why the property had not been realised, and, once that thought has crossed the consciousness, it is difficult to suppress completely the suspicion that abandonment might have taken place. But this is to speculate.

For love favour and affection

Gratuitous dispositions between family members are common. The familiar formula takes just seconds to write: 'for love favour and affection'. Such trans-actions may have many attractions: the absence of missives, and of trench warfare over title queries, building warrants and so on. For the clients there is the attraction of no stamp duty. But behind all this lurks a danger. If both (i) there is in fact a consideration of some kind, and (ii) the disponer is later sequestrated, then major problems may emerge. The trustee in sequestration naturally challenges the transfer as a gratuitous alienation. The defender says that the transaction was in truth onerous, but the trustee responds by pointing to that damning formula: 'love favour and affection'. The legal question which arises is whether such a statement is conclusive, or whether it is open to the disponee to offer evidence to show that it was false. The practical issue is how allegedly gratuitous transfers should be handled.

There were two cases in this area in 2000.[1] In *Nottay's Trustee* v *Nottay*[2] Mohinder Singh Nottay and Rashpal Kaur Nottay, spouses, were co-owners of 56 Moat View, Roslin, Midlothian. In 1996 Singh disponed to Rashpal his half share, the disposition narrating that it was for love favour and affection. The following year he was sequestrated. The disposition had every appearance of a challengeable gratuitous alienation. For reasons which do not appear from Lord Clarke's judgment, the trustee in sequestration did not seek reduction but instead sought payment of the sum of £6,700.[3] How that sum was arrived at is not apparent.

The defence was that the statement in the disposition was untrue, and that Rashpal had in fact given adequate consideration. Before the disposition there

---

1 For a similar case last year see *Aitken's Trustee* v *Aitken* 1999 GWD 39–1898 (*Conveyancing 1999 Case* (68)).
2 2000 GWD 28–1091.
3 He also sought payment of £12,000 in respect of an alleged gratuitous alienation by the debtor to his wife of certain machines.

had been two loans secured on the property, from the Halifax and from Cedar Holdings, amounting to £37,647.52 and £14,254 respectively. After the disposition she had remortgaged with the Bank of Scotland in her sole name and with the proceeds paid off those debts. The bankrupt's share of those debts had been one half, so she had paid off £25,950.76 for him, plus certain other debts, making a grand total of £28,998.76. That amount was rather more than one half of the market value of the property as a whole. Hence she had given full value.

This was an interesting defence, but the pursuer challenged its relevancy. The disposition was expressly declared to have been gratuitous, and that was conclusive. The defender averred that she intended to seek judicial rectification of the disposition, so as to substitute the words 'certain good and onerous causes' for the words 'love favour and affection' but a mere alleged intention of this sort could not be listened to.

The Lord Ordinary (Clarke) held that the defence was relevant and that proof of the defender's averments should be allowed. Two authorities in particular were relied on, *Matheson's Trustee* v *Matheson*[1] and *McFadyen's Trustee* v *McFadyen*.[2] In the latter case an application for rectification had in fact already been made, and so the present case goes further.

Bank of Scotland v *Reid*[3] was a similar case. Jean Reid was the owner of Logieburn Farm near Elgin. In 1979 she leased the farm to her son, Alexander. In 1995 Alexander assigned the lease to his daughter, Jill. The narrative clause stated that the deed was gratuitous.[4] In 1996 Alexander was sequestrated. Later, an action was raised to reduce the assignation as a gratuitous alienation.[5] The defence was that the narrative clause was untrue, since the disponee had in fact made a lump-sum payment to the disponer and had also waived a claim against him. It was held that the defender was entitled to go to proof on these averments. The question of whether the narrative clause could be contradicted was argued, but was not brought into quite as sharp a focus as in *Nottay*.

The willingness of the court to admit evidence contradicting the narrative clause in a case of this sort contrasts markedly with an unwillingness to do so in disputes involving destinations[6] and, most recently, actions of division and sale.[7] There seem to be separate streams of authority: for example in *Nottay* the case law on the parallel issue for special destinations is not mentioned. It may be doubted whether the law is coherent. There seems no reason why a narrative clause should be regarded as conclusive and incapable of being contradicted in certain cases but as non-conclusive and capable of being contradicted in other cases.

---

1 1992 SLT 685.
2 1994 SLT 416.
3 2000 GWD 22–858.
4 In fact it did not use the 'love favour and affection' formula. The formula was 'without any payment to me'.
5 Unusually, the action was not at the instance of the trustee in sequestration but of a creditor. The Bank of Scotland held a standard security over the *dominium utile*.
6 See for example *Gordon-Rodgers* v *Thomson's Executors* 1998 SC 145.
7 *McCafferty* v *McCafferty* 2000 SCLR 256 (digested earlier as Case (8)).

Finally, practicalities. When clients state that something is being done gratuitously it is easy to accept that statement as a fact. It may, however, be wise to probe a little, and it will certainly be wise to have on file evidence on what the clients instructed. It sometimes happens that clients label a transfer as gratuitous because it is not a sale and because the parties are family members. But the fact that the parties are family members and the transfer is not a sale does not necessarily mean that it is gratuitous. There may well be some sort of consideration in the background. The wooden use of 'love favour and affection' may turn out to prejudice the interests of the grantee. Narrative clauses can, and should, be crafted to suit the occasion. It should be added that, as mentioned earlier, an affidavit of solvency from the disponer will assist in the future marketability of the property.

RIGHT-TO-BUY LEGISLATION

What happens if a tenant applies to buy his/her property but it turns out that part of it has already been sold to the neighbour?

In *Higgins* v *North Lanarkshire Council*[1] Mr Higgins and Mrs Sloan were neighbours, at 8 and 12 Livingstone Place, Airdie. Both were council tenants, and, having secure tenancies, both had the right to buy. Each had a piece of garden ground. Mrs Sloan applied to buy her property. The transaction duly settled. Mrs Sloan was registered as proprietor in the Land Register with no exclusion of indemnity. But Mr Higgins was not happy. In the disposition by the Council to Mrs Sloan, and thus in her title sheet, was a strip of land which Mr Higgins considered to be part of the garden effeiring to his property, though it was physically part of Mrs Sloan's garden.[2] When he discovered that the Council was proposing to convey this strip to Mrs Sloan, Mr Higgins got his solicitor to write to the Council to object. But his protests were unavailing.

Mr Higgins then applied to buy his property. The Council responded by an offer to sell, but the property offered did not include the strip of ground in question. Mr Higgins regarded that as unacceptable, and, as was his right, he applied to the Lands Tribunal. His position was that the strip of ground had always been part of the property as let to him, and that he had allowed Mrs Sloan the use of it as a matter of grace and favour only. Apparently it was useful for parking. The Tribunal undertook a detailed factual investigation, and came to the conclusion that Mr Higgins was right. The strip was in his let, not in Mrs Sloan's let. Therefore in terms of the legislation he was entitled to have it included in the property which the Council offered to sell to him.

But at this point an obvious difficulty emerged, and was strongly urged by the Council. The Council no longer owned the strip. So they could not convey it

---

1 2000 GWD 31–1236. The members of the Tribunal for this case were R A Edwards WS and A R MacLeary FRICS.
2 The account given here is a slightly a simplified version. The details are fully explored in the painstaking opinion of the Tribunal.

to Mr Higgins: one cannot transfer what one does not have— *nemo plus juris ad alium transferre potest quam ipse haberet*. This was not the first time the issue had been before the Tribunal. In two cases reported in 1987, *Popescu v Banff and Buchan District Council*[1] and *Morrison v Stirling District Council*[2] the Tribunal took the view that the landlords were bound to sell what the tenant was entitled to buy, and it was no defence that part of the property had been sold to a neighbour. But later the Tribunal changed its mind, in an unreported case in 1994 called *Brown v Scottish Homes*.[3] The reason for the change was reliance on certain remarks from the Inner House in two cases, *Ross and Cromarty District Council v Patience*[4] and *City of Glasgow District Council v Doyle*[5] both indicating that there was no right to buy what the landlord did not own. But the *Patience* decision was later reversed in the House of Lords.[6]

In *Higgins* the Council, influenced chiefly by the House of Lords' decision in *Patience*, decided to revert to its older rule. A landlord is bound to sell what the tenant is entitled to buy. It was not true, observed the Tribunal, that the effect of the decision would be to require the landlord to do something impossible. After all, in the ordinary case it can happen that sellers are bound by missives to convey more than they have. If that happens, the sellers must manage, by one means or another, to procure the title, which failing damages will be presumptively payable. The effect of the order granted in favour of Mr Higgins would not put the Council in a worse position than the ordinary case just described.

The Tribunal, having made that decision, said a great deal more. In the course of its factual investigation about the disputed strip, it had come to the conclusion that Mrs Sloan had not been blameless in the matter. The Tribunal found that 'it is ... difficult to resist the conclusion that she suppressed the agreement she had evidently come to with Mr Higgins regarding the disputed land when she met Mr Smyth[7] on site, and so caused him to come to the conclusion that the disputed land should be conveyed to her.' This being so, the Tribunal took the view that what has come to be known as the 'offside goals rule' was applicable.[8] The Council had conveyed to Mrs Sloan in breach of its obligation to convey to Mr Higgins. Mrs Sloan knew this. She was thus in bad faith. Hence her title to the disputed strip was a voidable title.[9]

The Tribunal's analysis is careful and interesting, although whether it is correct is uncertain. At the time when the Council conveyed to Mrs Sloan, they were not yet under an obligation to convey to Mr Higgins, because the latter

1 1987 SLT (Lands Tr) 20.
2 1987 SLT (Lands Tr) 22.
3 5 May 1994.
4 1995 SC 382. In the *Patience* case the landlord's title was burdened by a pre-emption clause.
5 1993 SLT 604.
6 1997 SC (HL) 46.
7 Mr Smyth was a council official who visited the site and met both Mrs Sloan and Mr Higgins.
8 For this subject see K G C Reid, *The Law of Property in Scotland* (1996) para 695 *et seq*.
9 This still left open the difficulty of how the reduction was to be given effect to on the Land Register. That aspect of the decision is discussed further below, in the context of registration of title.

had not yet invoked his right to buy. It is true that the Council had a potential obligation to convey to Mr Higgins, but it seems open to question whether a mere potential obligation is sufficient to bring the offside goals rule into operation.

It should be noted that if the Council had granted Mrs Sloan absolute warrandice (which they seem to have done), they would be *prima facie* liable to her under that warrandice in the event that her title to the disputed strip was set aside.

REGISTRATION OF TITLE

Becoming owner

Registration of title theory holds that title flows from the Land Register, and not from the underlying deeds. Once a person is entered on the Register as owner of certain land, then he is, as a matter of law, the owner and there is no need to look further. So far as the Land Register is concerned, what you see is what you get.[1] Subject to certain qualifications, there is no such thing as a void registration. There is such a thing as a registration which should not have been made, and such a registration may be 'rectifiable'. But 'rectifiable' does not mean void. The legislative basis of this principle is s 3(1)(a) of the Land Registration (Scotland) Act 1979, which provides that registration has the effect of 'vesting in the person registered as entitled to the registered interest in land a real right in and to the interest . . .'

The full implications of this principle—novel, or even startling, for those brought up with the Register of Sasines—are only now beginning to be worked out. An example arose in *Summers* v *Crichton*.[2] This was a dispute between two neighbours as to the ownership of some land. The defender's title was on the Land Register, while the pursuer's remained on the Register of Sasines. In principle such a dispute ought to be easily resolved. A person with a registered title owns whatever the Land Register says he owns. There is no room for argument. So it is simply a matter of looking at the land certificate. It is true that an entry on the Register can be attacked as inaccurate, and rectification sought. But unless and until that is done, the entry represents the position in law. As Lord President Rodger put it in another case from 2000, *Keeper of the Registers of Scotland* v *M R S Hamilton Ltd*:[3]

> [T]he information contained in the title sheet may not in fact be accurate. But that does not affect the position—unless and until the Keeper rectifies the Register. Unless and until that happens, the proprietor is vested in the interest as it is to be found in the title sheet.

Accordingly, if (as was apparently the case) the disputed land was shown as part of the defender's registered title, then it was indeed her property. The fact

---

1 See further G L Gretton and K G C Reid, *Conveyancing* (2nd edn, 1999) para 8.02.
2 2000 GWD 40–1495.
3 2000 SLT 352 at 357B.

that the pursuer's Sasine title might also indicate ownership of the land would then be irrelevant.[1]

Oddly, an argument along these lines was rejected by the Lord Ordinary (Lord Cameron of Lochbroom). Admittedly, there was a difficulty with the pleadings. But Lord Cameron seems to have taken the view that s 3(1) of the Land Registration (Scotland) Act 1979 is qualified by s 7:[2]

> [S]ection 7(3) . . . provides that a title to a registered interest and a title governed by a deed recorded in the Register of Sasines should rank according to the respective dates of registration and recording. This suggests that an indefeasible right attached to each title at least until reduction or rectification took place.

The effect of Lord Cameron's analysis is to put Sasine titles on the same footing as Land Register titles. But with respect, this is based on a misunderstanding of s 7.[3]

Section 7 is headed 'ranking'. Ranking occurs only between compatible rights—in practice between heritable securities. But two ownerships cannot rank with each other. If the pursuer is owner, the defender is not. Or if the defender is owner, the pursuer is not. They cannot both be owners, one postponed to the other. Section 7, therefore, is irrelevant to disputes as to ownership.[4]

Remaining owner

By registration a person becomes owner. But he will not necessarily *remain* owner. For a person to cease to be owner, however, it is necessary that his name be removed from the Register.[5] Usually such removal is voluntary, brought about by the registered owner transferring the property to someone else. But the 1979 Act also envisages involuntary removal in cases where the Register is 'inaccurate'—where, in other words, the entry on the Register was not justified by the underlying deed. Involuntary removal is accomplished by rectification; but rectification can proceed against a proprietor in possession only in very limited circumstances.[6] The only important cases are where indemnity has been excluded by the Keeper, or where the inaccuracy was caused by the proprietor's fraud or carelessness. So limited are these circumstances, indeed, that rectification is almost unknown, at least as far as the reported cases are

---

1 Except perhaps in support of an application for rectification.
2 Para 6 of the transcript.
3 K G C Reid, '*A Non Domino* Conveyances and the Land Register' 1991 *Juridical Review* 79 at 86; G L Gretton and K G C Reid, *Conveyancing* (2nd edn, 1999) para 8.15.
4 The pursuer is seeking a declarator of ownership. If he is ultimately successful, the result of the approach adopted by Lord Cameron will be that the court will be declaring as owner a person other than the person entered as owner on the Land Register. That in turn would mean that the Land Register could no longer be relied upon as showing the owner of land.
5 Unless, by error, two title sheets overlap and the same area of ground is included in both. There are then two rival claimants for ownership, and it is not clear how the competition would be resolved.
6 Land Registration (Scotland) Act 1979, s 9(3).

concerned. If rectification is barred, the remedy of the wronged party is indemnity from the Keeper.[1]

Stevenson-Hamilton's Exrs v *McStay (No 2)*[2] is a rare example of a case in which rectification was granted. The facts are instructive. A gap site at 81 Clyde Street, Carluke, was part of an estate belonging to the executors (the pursuers in the action). In September 1983 John McStay granted an *a non domino* disposition of the site to his wife. The disposition was duly recorded in the Register of Sasines. Thereafter there were occasional acts of possession, but not enough—it was held in the current litigation—to constitute possession for the purposes of positive prescription. Nonetheless, in December 1993—10 years later—Mrs McStay granted a disposition of the property to herself and her husband, and an application was made to the Land Register for registration. The application was supported by affidavits from the applicants and a neighbour to the effect that there had been open and peaceable possession for 10 years. On this basis the Keeper accepted the application and registered the McStays without exclusion of indemnity.

Who was owner? Had the property still been in the Register of Sasines, the executors would have still been the owners. This is because the disposition to Mrs McStay was granted *a non domino* and had not been followed by prescriptive possession. But by registration in the Land Register the McStays had converted a void title into one which, even if challengeable, was not void. Registration confers ownership even on the unworthy. The Register, however, was inaccurate, for the 1993 disposition was also granted *a non domino* and did not justify the entry on the Register. Accordingly, the executors sought reduction of the disposition and rectification of the Register.

There was no difficulty about the reduction.[3] But (indemnity not having been excluded), rectification could be granted only if the McStays had been fraudulent or careless. The Lord Ordinary (T G Coutts QC) held that there had been fraud or carelessness. The answers to some of the questions in the form 1 were false. In the current version of the form, these were questions 3,[4] 13[5] and 14.[6] 'If not deliberately false, it was at the least careless.'[7] Accordingly, an order for rectification was granted. The end result, therefore, was the same as in Sasine cases: the executors were owners.

Finally, it may be noted that the position would have been different if, before the executors realised what had happened, the McStays had sold the

---

1 1979 Act, s 12(1)(b). And see below.
2 2000 GWD 22–872.
3 But in Land Register cases a reduction is of limited value without rectification. Without rectification the defender remains on the Register as owner. See *Short's Tr* v *Keeper of the Registers of Scotland* 1996 SC (HL) 14.
4 'Is there any person in possession or occupation of the subjects or any part of them adversely to the interest of the applicant?'
5 'Are the deeds and documents detailed in the Inventory (Form 4) all the deeds and documents relevant to the title?'
6 'Are there any facts and circumstances material to the right or title of the applicant which have not already been disclosed in this application or its accompanying documents?'
7 Transcript para 21.

property on. A purchaser would be entitled to rely on the Register, and would not examine the underlying deeds. The Register disclosed the McStays as owners. Hence, a purchaser would be neither fraudulent nor careless. The executors would have been unable to recover the property. Presumably they would have had a claim against the McStays either in delict or in unjustified enrichment. Alternatively, they would have had a claim against the Keeper for refusal to rectify.[1]

Another case touching on rectification was *Higgins* v *North Lanarkshire Council*.[2] Mrs Sloan was registered as owner, without exclusion of indemnity, of a house and garden, including a strip which was part of property let to her neighbour, Mr Higgins, on a secure tenancy. It was held by the Lands Tribunal that Mr Higgins was entitled to buy this strip under the right-to-buy legislation, and that Mrs Sloan had scored an 'offside goal' by inducing the Council to convey it to her. If that was right, it would follow that Mrs Sloan's disposition was voidable in so far as it conveyed the strip.

Had this been a Sasine case, the procedure would have been for Mr Higgins to reduce the disposition to Mrs Sloan, *quoad excessum*, and to record the extract decree of reduction. That having been done, the Council would then have conveyed the strip to Mr Higgins. But this being a Land Register case, the Tribunal took the view that no action of reduction would be necessary. The Register was inaccurate by virtue of the simple fact that Mrs Sloan had scored an offside goal. As she was a proprietor in possession and as there was no exclusion of indemnity, it might seem that the inaccuracy was a non-rectifiable inaccuracy. But such a conclusion, the Tribunal argued, would be mistaken. The inaccuracy had been caused substantially by the fraud or carelessness of Mrs Sloan. That being so, her protection against rectification disappeared.[3] Accordingly, the Keeper was free to go ahead and rectify without more ado.

This analysis may not pay sufficient attention to s 9 of the Land Registration (Scotland) Act 1979. Section s 9(1) allows rectification only if there is an 'inaccuracy in the register'. Although the concept of inaccuracy is an important one, its meaning is not explained in the 1979 Act. A standard view is that an entry is inaccurate if it was not justified by the deed or deeds which induced registration, or if something has happened since registration which means that the entry, though once accurate, has become inaccurate.[4] If that is right, the registration in favour of Mrs Sloan was not inaccurate at the time of registration. It would become inaccurate upon reduction of the disposition, but not before.

---

1 In which case the Keeper would presumably have been subrogated to their claim against the McStays.
2 2000 GWD 31–1236 (Lands Tr). The members of the Tribunal for this case were R A Edwards WS and A R MacLeary FRICS. Other aspects of this case were analysed above under the heading of Right-to-Buy.
3 Land Registration (Scotland) Act 1979, s 9(3)(a)(iii).
4 G L Gretton and K G C Reid, *Conveyancing* (2nd edn, 1999) para 8.07. In *Short's Tr* v *Keeper of the Registers* 1994 SC 122, when that case was in the Inner House, Lord President Hope said (at p 122) that 'an entry is inaccurate if it appears that at the time it was made or in the light of subsequent events it ought not to have been made'.

So long as the disposition in favour of Mrs Sloan stood unreduced, therefore, the registration could not be challenged.[1]

Indemnity

The decision of the First Division in *Keeper of the Registers of Scotland* v *M R S Hamilton*[2] settles an issue concerning indemnity which has been disputed for some time. Section 12(1) of the Land Registration (Scotland) Act 1979 provides that:

> Subject to the provisions of this section, a person who suffers loss as a result of—
>
> (a) a rectification of the register made under section 9 of this Act;
> (b) the refusal or omission of the Keeper to make such a rectification;
> (c) the loss or destruction of any document while lodged with the Keeper;
> (d) an error or omission in any land or charge certificate given by the Keeper in writing or in such other manner as may be prescribed by rules made under section 27 of this Act,
>
> shall be entitled to be indemnified by the Keeper in respect of that loss.

The difficulty concerns paragraph (d). Here two different meanings seem possible. A narrow interpretation is that there is an error or omission in a land certificate only where the certificate is actually different from the title sheet. In other words, it is not an accurate copy of the title sheet. A wide interpretation is that even a faithful copy is erroneous if the title sheet itself was erroneous. If, for example, the title sheet omitted a standard security, and the land certificate accurately reproduced the title sheet, then, in this view, the land certificate would be erroneous under paragraph (d).

The difference matters. Indemnity is normally claimed under either paragraph (a) or paragraph (b) of s 12(1)—more usually under paragraph (b). But these provisions may not fully indemnify a claimant. A person who claims under paragraph (b)—as the pursuer originally did in the present case—is entitled only to be put into the position he would have been in had the Keeper in fact rectified the Register on the date he was requested to do so. That date may be many years after the inaccurate entry was first made. For these lost years there is no compensation.[3] Further, paragraphs (a) and (b) are restrictive in relation to parties as well as to quantum. In practice only someone who is refused

---

1 It is also possible to argue that, since rectification involves the deprivation of property, and since the right to property is protected by article 1 of the First Protocol of the European Convention on Human Rights, any rectification without a judicial process which involves the owner in question would be a breach of article 6 (right to a fair trial). But this is speculative.

2 2000 SC 271, 2000 SLT 352.

3 To avoid this difficulty the pursuer argued that the effect of rectification is retrospective, back to the date of the original erroneous registration. But retrospective rectification would render the registration system self-contradictory, and this argument failed. The same restricted indemnity occurs where the Keeper grants rectification rather than refusing it. The successful applicant is restored to his proper position from that date. There is no provision for indemnity for the lost years when the Register was inaccurate.

rectification is likely to be able to claim indemnity under paragraph (b). Third parties will be excluded.

Paragraph (d) would, on a wide interpretation, offer much more generous terms. *Any* loss caused by an error or omission in the Register would be recoverable, and by any person.

At first instance, the Lands Tribunal adopted the wide interpretation of paragraph (d). The same conclusion had previously been reached by Lord Hamilton in *M R S Hamilton* v *Keeper of the Registers of Scotland (No 1)*.[1] But that view has now been rejected—surely correctly—by the First Division. A wide interpretation of paragraph (d) would render paragraph (b) otiose. And there is no reason to suppose that Parliament intended such a wide basis of indemnity. In any event, the drafting of paragraph (d) was, in the Lord President's view, clear. With this decision the issue may now be taken as settled.

Salmon fishings and the refusal of registration

The excellent new edition of the *Registration of Title Practice Book* states:[2]

> It is not uncommon for the owner of a right in salmon fishings to convey a *pro indiviso* share or shares in that right to some other party or parties. Such conveyances are, of course, wholly competent and the interest will be given effect to in the Land Register. However, some such conveyances contain clauses that restrict the right to fish for salmon to a set number of rods in a particular beat during a designated week(s). These conveyances provide that the disponee is barred from making any use of that part of the fishings at any other time in the year and of the remainder of the fishings at any time at all. The Keeper considers that such qualifications on occupation and exercise of the right are inconsistent with the unrestricted nature of a real right of common ownership. Consequently, the Keeper's policy, which was reached after consultation with the Joint Consultative Committee (November 1999), is to reject any application for registration which is founded on such a conveyance.

This decision—which, it is understood, is being applied not only to the Land Register but also to the Register of Sasines—has caused concern in some quarters, and there is the possibility that it will be challenged in the courts.[3]

Timeshares, whether of holiday cottages or of fishing rights, can be and have been set up in a number of different ways. One method is to vest ownership in a trustee, so that those who buy timeshares hold transferable beneficial interests in a trust. If that is done, the timesharing happens outwith the Land Register or Register of Sasines. With arrangements of that sort the Keeper has no problem. But some timeshares have been done in a different way. Each buyer receives a *pro indiviso* share. There is a deed of conditions which purports to impose real burdens on each share. The burdens will regulate times of use, and so on. It is this sort of timeshare which the Keeper is concerned about.

---

1 1999 SLT 829.

2 (2nd edn, 2000) para 6–106.

3 See the note by Malcolm Strang Steel in the August 2000 issue of the *Journal of the Law Society of Scotland*. In the same issue there is a note by Alistair Rennie defending the Keeper's position.

The Keeper's statement that 'such qualifications on occupation and exercise of the right are inconsistent with the unrestricted nature of a real right of common ownership' seems correct. Co-owners are perfectly free *by contract* to regulate times of use. But such provisions would probably be held to be incapable of binding singular successors. In other words, such burdens may be personal, but probably not real. As Lord Young said: 'You cannot make a man proprietor and yet prohibit him [by means of real burdens] from exercising the rights of proprietorship.'[1] Real burdens can go so far, but no further. Of course, in a sense any real burden encroaches upon absolute ownership. It is a question of proportion. A real burden forbidding commercial use is acceptable. A real burden forbidding use or possession for 51 weeks a year is probably not.[2]

But, with respect, the consequence for such timeshare arrangements is simply that and no more: the burdens, while they may be valid contractually, probably do not bind singular successors. That may be unfortunate for those involved, but it is not in legal terms a specially remarkable result. By no means all purported real burdens are valid. Whether to enter into the title sheet burdens which are probably invalid is a problem which must face the Keeper every day. The fact that a title comes with probably invalid burdens is no ground for refusing to register it.[3] If it were, the title to many properties would be un-registrable. Hence, it is respectfully suggested that the Keeper's analysis of this issue is one which could usefully be revisited.[4]

Reform

It has been announced that the Scottish Law Commission is to review the 1979 Act as part of its new programme of law reform.[5] A consultation paper will be issued in due course, but no doubt it will be several years before amending legislation is passed.

---

1 *Moir's Trs* v *McEwan* (1880) 7 R 1141 at 1145.
2 Apart from this issue as to content, there is a problem as to form. It is not certain whether it is competent for one *pro indiviso* share to be subject to a real burden in favour of another *pro indiviso* share. For discussion see K G C Reid, *The Law of Property in Scotland* (1996) para 411. There are some *dicta* by Lord Hope in *Clydesdale Bank* v *Davidson* 1998 SC (HL) 51 indicating that the problem of form may be fatal. The Scottish Law Commission has recommended that in future it should not be possible for *pro indiviso* shares to be, as such, subject to real burdens: see *Report on Real Burdens* (Scot Law Com No 181) para 3.2.
3 The Keeper takes the view that he cannot enter into a title sheet an invalid burden: see the note in the August 2001 issue of the *Journal of the Law Society of Scotland* (citing s 6(1)(e) of the 1979 Act). In that case he should simply omit them. But in fact the inclusion of a purported real burden is in any event no guarantee of its validity.
4 But it seems undeniable that arrangements of this sort are undesirable. From the private point of view such arrangements are flawed because the burdens are probably not valid as real burdens, and also because of the possibility that any single co-proprietor could raise an action of division and sale. And from the public point of view, the fragmentation of a single unit into dozens or sometimes hundreds of separate registrable micro-units is something which one suspects that the framers of the Land Registration (Scotland) Act 1979 would have disallowed, had they foreseen it.
5 Scottish Law Commission, *Sixth Programme of Law Reform* (Scot Law Com No 176, 2000) paras 2.13 to 2.17.

SOLICITORS AND ESTATE AGENTS

Liability to lender for failure to disclose information?

Leeds & Holbeck Building Society v *Alex Morison & Co* was a negligence action, the first round of which was reported last year.[1] A proof before answer was allowed, and this has now taken place.[2]

Mr and Mrs Prendiville were a London couple with an interest in tennis. Through tennis they got to know a partner in a Scottish firm of solicitors, and they retained him as their solicitor when they bought Blanerne House, near Duns, in 1986. Their mortgage was with the Newcastle Building Society. In 1990 they remortgaged with the Leeds & Holbeck Building Society, the loan being £373,488 at 15.7% for a term of 18 years. The same solicitor acted in that transaction, and he acted also for the building society. The Prendivilles defaulted almost at once, and the building society sold the property for only £200,000. It seems that they were unable to recover the shortfall from the Prendivilles. In a move which nowadays is increasingly common, they sued the firm of solicitors for the sum of £458,055.46.[3] The ground of action was negligence. The loan was on the express basis, warranted by the Prendivilles, that the property was for residential use. However, the truth was that the Prendivilles were at the time making vigorous attempts to redevelop the property into a tennis-themed hotel. They had obtained planning permission, and were engaged in negotiations for commercial funding. Had all gone to plan, within a matter of a few months of the remortgage with the building society there would have been yet another remortgage with a commercial lender.

The building society's position was that had they known of the Prendivilles' plans they would not have lent them the money. Although the defenders questioned this, it was accepted by the court. It should be noted that the issue concerned only the Prendivilles' *plans*. At the time of the remortgage the property was residential and indeed it remained so. This was thus not one of those cases where a loan is obtained over commercial property on the false representation that it is residential property.

The key question, therefore, was whether the solicitor, who knew of the Prendivilles' intentions, should have told the building society. Both sides led expert evidence as to proper conveyancing practice. Lady Paton took the view that, whilst the solicitor knew of the Prendivilles' plans, he also knew that they were unrealistic and unlikely to come to anything, a belief that was confirmed by events. That being so, he was under no obligation to tell the building society.

The outcome is surely right. Nevertheless, it is arguable that the action ought to have failed much earlier, on the basic issue of relevancy. In the absence of a special request, why should a solicitor have to tell the lender about mere plans for the future? It is difficult to see what wrong is done by the mere intentions.

---

1 1999 GWD 9–434, and see *Conveyancing 1999* p 74.
2 2001 SCLR 41.
3 We are unclear how that remarkable figure was arrived at.

These were *not* intentions to breach the contract with the Leeds & Holbeck. An intention to obtain a loan on a residential basis and then convert the property to commercial use *while keeping the residential loan in place* might amount to fraud. But it does not seem that that was what the Prendivilles intended. It does not seem that the Prendivilles were guilty of any misrepresentation, or of any breach of contract (except, of course, eventual default on the loan) or of any anticipatory breach of contract, nor does it seem that they intended any such breach.

We are now left with the ruling of the Lord Ordinary at debate, and confirmed by Lady Paton, that if the solicitor had not thought that the Prendivilles' plans were unrealistic he *would* have been under an obligation to inform the lenders. The issue is one of great practical importance. Solicitors often hear much from their clients, including their possible plans. If this decision is correct law agents must be constantly thinking whether they should let the client's lender know of such plans. The sanction for failing to do so may prove to be that the solicitor becomes, in effect, a cautioner for the mortgage loan. Whether this can really be the law seems doubtful. But that seems to be the implication arising from *Leeds & Holbeck*.

Naturally, the case also illustrates the dangers of acting for both borrower and lender, a practice much less common today than in 1990.

A subsidiary but important issue in the case was causality. The pursuers argued that the solicitor had been in breach of his duty, and that if he had not been in breach then they would never have made the unfortunate loan to the Prendivilles, and so would have avoided loss. Hence their loss was caused by his breach of duty. In response, the defenders cited a well-known English case in the House of Lords, *Banque Bruxelles Lambert S.A.* v *Eagle Star Insurance Co. Ltd*,[1] and especially the speech of Lord Hoffmann:[2]

> A mountaineer about to undertake a difficult climb is concerned about the fitness of his knee. He goes to a doctor who negligently makes a superficial examination and pronounces the knee fit. The climber goes on the expedition, which he would not have undertaken if the doctor had told him the true state of his knee. He suffers an injury which is an entirely foreseeable consequence of mountaineering but has nothing to do with his knee. On the Court of Appeal's principle, the doctor is responsible for the injury suffered by the mountaineer because it is damage which would not have occurred if he had been given correct information about his knee. He would not have gone on the expedition and would have suffered no injury. On what I have suggested is the more usual principle, the doctor is not liable. The injury has not been caused by the doctor's bad advice because it would have occurred even if the advice had been correct.

In *Leeds & Holbeck* the defenders argued that this was precisely in point. Whilst it might be true that the building society would not have lent had they known of the Prendivilles' plans, that is not enough to establish causality. The test is this: would the loss have happened 'even if the advice had been correct'? As

---

1 [1997] AC 191.
2 Pages 213–214.

applied to the facts of *Leeds & Holbeck*, that means that the question was whether the building society would have still suffered the loss even if the Prendivilles had had no commercial intentions. The answer to that question is presumably affirmative. If that is so, then on Lord Hoffmann's test the defenders were not liable, even if the solicitor had been in breach of duty. Surprisingly, Lady Paton did not accept that argument.

Although the defenders were successful, this case must be regarded with considerable concern by the legal profession, and it is respectfully suggested that whilst the final outcome was correct, the pursuers' case was bad in law and should have been rejected for that reason.

Finally, by way of postscript, it may be doubted whether the nature of a solicitor's obligation should be the same for every class of lender. Why should it be assumed that a solicitor owes the same duties regardless of the client? The standard applied in *Leeds & Holbeck* was the one laid down in the celebrated case of *Hunter* v *Hanley*,[1] namely the standard of the 'ordinarily competent solicitor exercising reasonable care and skill'. But what such a solicitor will or will not do may depend on a variety of contextual factors, including the issue of what sort of client is in question. It is suggested that the *Hunter* v *Hanley* standard should be more strict where a security is being taken for a private client without lending experience—and therefore less strict in the case of a professional moneylender.

Limitations to the Master Policy?

In *Cheltenham & Gloucester Building Society* v *Royal & Sun Alliance Insurance*[2] the pursuers instructed a solicitor to take a 'first charge' over certain property. He failed to do so, there being a prior security in favour of the Bank of Scotland. As a result a debt of £131,696.14 due by the borrowers could not be recovered. But recovery against the solicitor proved impossible in view of his sequestration. The Third Parties (Rights against Insurers) Act 1930 provides that in such a case a direct action against the insurers is competent. Accordingly, the building society sued Royal & Sun Alliance, the insurers under the Master Policy. The latter pointed out that they were entitled to avail themselves of any restrictions there might be in the policy.

The policy provided:

> The Insurers will indemnify the Insured . . . against liability at law for damages and claimant's costs and expenses in respect of claims . . . made against the insured . . . by reason of any negligent act neglect or omission on the part of the . . . insured . . . occurring or committed . . . *in good faith* . . .[3]

The defenders argued (in the words of the Lord Ordinary, Lord Carloway) 'that the insured had not acted in good faith in that he knew of the prior security held

---

1 1955 SC 200.
2 2000 GWD 32–1253.
3 Emphasis added.

by the Bank of Scotland and had acted deliberately in not obtaining its discharge before advising the pursuers about the purported satisfactory completion of the security arrangements'. Proof was allowed.

The case is a useful reminder that the Master Policy has its limitations. The border between mere negligence and actual bad faith may sometimes be a narrow one.

Section 16 of the Succession (Scotland) Act 1964

In *Paul v Ogilvy*[1] Thomas Paul had a lease of Kessington Farm near Bearsden. He died in January 1990. Under s 16 of the Succession (Scotland) Act 1964 his executors were bound within 12 months to intimate to the landlords who the successor to the lease would be. This was not done. As a result the landlords exercised their right to terminate the lease.[2] The solicitor acting for the executors admitted liability for having failed to ensure that the s 16 procedure was timeously carried through. The case was about quantum. The land had potential development value. In the event of a favourable change of planning consents both landlords and tenants would have benefited, and indeed Alfred McAlpine Homes Scotland Limited were interested. The problem was how the damages should reflect the development potential. On the basis of evidence that there was a 30% chance of a favourable planning outcome, the Lord Ordinary (Hamilton) awarded 30% of the sum which a developer could be expected to have paid for an assignation of the lease if the planning outcome had been favourable. The latter figure was £750,000. Hence, the damages payable in that respect were £180,604. There was a 70% chance that planning permission would not have been granted, and so the value of the lease without change of planning permission was also due by way of damages, but not the full amount, just 70% of it. This value was estimated at £50,000, 70% of which was £35,000. These figures were then subject to certain adjustments, and the final figure for the damages awarded was £286,600.

The case is one of considerable importance in the law relating to the computation of damages. More immediately, it is a reminder of the dangers of overlooking s 16 of the 1964 Act.

JUDICIAL RECTIFICATION

In conveyancing, when all else fails, it is often worth considering the possibility of judicial rectification. By s 8 of the Law Reform (Miscellaneous Provisions) (Scotland) Act 1985 the court (including the sheriff court) is empowered to rectify documents which fail to express accurately the parties' intentions. What the conveyancer has failed to achieve, therefore, can sometimes be achieved with the aid of the court. Since 1985 there has been a growing body of case law on s 8,

---

1 2001 SLT 171.
2 Section 16 was discussed at pp 63–66 in the context of another case from 2000, *Sproat v South West Services (Galloway) Ltd* 2000 GWD 37–1416.

and all the standard conveyancing deeds have been the subject of rectification, including dispositions and standard securities. In general, the approach of the courts has been to take a broad and creative view of s 8 and not to refuse rectification merely on some technical ground.[1]

Right words, wrong result

That approach is continued in an important new case, *Bank of Ireland* v *Bass Brewers Ltd*.[2] Rectification applications are usually concerned with errors in expression, that is to say with wrong words or omitted words. But there may also be an error in *expectation*. Parties may use words in the expectation that they will have a particular legal effect, but that expectation may then turn out to be misplaced. In such a case the deed uses the right words, but achieves the wrong result. Can rectification help?

This issue arose directly in *Bank of Ireland*. A company called Lewis Lloyd Holdings Ltd granted a floating charge to Bass Brewers. The floating charge contained a negative pledge clause prohibiting the creation of any fixed security having priority in ranking over the floating charge. In 1997 Lewis bought property at Hazelburn, Campbeltown, with the help of a loan from the Bank of Ireland. Since, naturally, the loan was to be secured by a first-ranking standard security, Lewis obtained a letter of non-crystallisation and consent to the granting of the security from Bass. The letter read as follows:

> We confirm that we have no intention of appointing a receiver under the floating charge granted by [Lewis] and will not do so within the next 21 days. We consent to the granting of the Standard Security by [Lewis] in favour of [the Bank of Ireland] . . .

Subsequently, that and other securities became the subject of litigation in which it was held that the letter did no more than permit the standard security, and did nothing to disturb the ranking in the original negative pledge clause. In other words, the floating charge ranked before the standard security. See *Griffith and Powdrill (Receivers of Lewis Lloyd Holdings Ltd) Petrs*.[3]

This was unwelcome news for the Bank of Ireland. It responded by seeking judicial rectification of the letter of consent. There was no error as to the words used. The words were deliberately chosen. But the recent litigation showed them to be the wrong words. Up until then—or so it was averred—'it was the widespread belief amongst solicitors dealing in such transactions . . . that the effect of a letter of consent from a holder of a subsisting floating charge to the grant of a standard security would be to disapply any negative pledge and enable the standard security to rank in priority to the floating charge'. In signing the letter, Bass must have intended that the standard security rank first.

---

1 For an overview account, see G L Gretton and K G C Reid, *Conveyancing* (2nd edn, 1999) chapter 17.
2 2000 GWD 20–786 and 2000 GWD 28–1077 discussed earlier at pp 81–83.
3 1998 GWD 40–2037.

Accordingly, the letter failed to give effect to their intention and ought to be rectified.[1] The particular rectification sought was the addition of the words 'prior ranking' after the words 'We consent to the granting of'.

In reply it was argued for Bass that rectification was not available for errors in expectation. If the letter used the words which it was intended to use, that was the end of the matter. The fact that the words had a legal effect different from that which was intended was beside the point. Lord Macfadyen rejected this argument. He saw no difficulty with rectification in those circumstances:[2]

> To exclude rectification where the language used is the language that the grantor intended to use but the legal result is different from the legal result that the grantor intended to achieve would reduce the role of the remedy to little more than the correction of clerical errors. There is, in my view, no reason in the language of the provision to read it in such a narrow way.

It is not clear how far the principle goes. In *Bank of Ireland* it was at least debatable that the words used in the letter had the legal effect intended. The drafting might be classified as a narrow miss.[3] The position may be different if the miss is less narrow. If a conveyancer uses words which no reasonable person would imagine could have the legal effect intended, a court might be reluctant to carry out the necessary corrective conveyancing. Section 8 confers a purely discretionary power, and it is not a power which the court is bound to exercise. As was said in another recent case on rectification, '[t]here is a qualification inherent in most if not all general discretionary powers that they require to be exercised within reasonable limits'.[4]

Different parties as between document and prior agreement

Usually, rectification is sought under paragraph (a) of s 8(1) of the Law Reform (Miscellaneous Provisions) (Scotland) Act 1985, which requires the existence of a prior agreement. There are thus two separate elements: the document to be rectified, and the prior agreement (which need not be in writing); and rectification is available if it can be shown that the document fails to express or give effect to the common intention of the parties to the prior agreement.

---

1 The application was under para (b) of s 8(1), which deals mainly with the case of freestanding documents not in implement of a previous agreement.
2 Para 22 of the transcript.
3 *Baird v Drumpellier & Mount Vernon Estates Ltd (No 2)* 2000 GWD 12–427 might also be analysed as a case on error in expectation. Here the sellers of land deleted the good and marketable title provisions in an offer to purchase, apparently overlooking the fact that a guarantee of good and marketable title is always implied except where the *implied* guarantee is also deleted. It may be that the purchasers were under a similar misapprehension. If so, then the common intention of the parties—this was a s 8(1)(a) case—may have been that the sellers were not to guarantee the title, and that intention was not then achieved by the wording used in the missives. In fact the application failed on the basis that no case based on common intention was relevantly pled.
4 *Norwich Union Life Insurance Society v Tanap Investments VK Ltd* 1999 SLT 204 at 211G *per* Lord Penrose *affd* 2000 SC 515, 2000 SLT 819.

Usually the parties to the agreement are the same as the parties to the document. In *Delikes Ltd* v *Scottish & Newcastle plc,*[1] however, they were not. This, it was held, was fatal to an application under s 8(1)(a).[2]

This approach seems unduly restrictive.[3] There is no particular difficulty in reading the relevant provisions in the opposite sense. And it is not difficult to think of situations where the view taken in the present case will operate unfairly. Suppose, for example, that A concludes missives of sale with B. But A is a widow and title remains in the name of her late husband. Hence the disposition is granted by the executor. There is then a mismatch between missives and disposition. The granter of the latter is not a party to the former. Hence, on the authority of *Delikes,* rectification would not be possible in the event, for example, that the disposition conveys a larger area of land than was agreed to in the missives.

Who can defend?

Naturally, an application for rectification can be opposed by the other party or parties to the document. It can also be opposed by a third party who acted in prejudicial reliance on the document in its unrectified form, for such a party is given special privileges by s 9 of the Act. But what has hitherto been less clear is whether there is title to defend in a third party who will be adversely affected by rectification but who does not fall within s 9 of the Law Reform (Miscellaneous Provisions) (Scotland) Act 1985. In *Norwich Union Life Insurance Society* v *Tanap Investments VK Ltd (No 2)*[4] the answer was given in the affirmative. Such a person would have title and interest to enforce under the general law. There was no reason to suppose that the special rule set out in s 9 was intended to remove a right which would otherwise exist.

RESIDENTIAL CARE FOR THE ELDERLY

People live longer than they used to. If, during the last years of their lives, they are unable to look after themselves, they may become a financial burden on those who care for them. The younger generation, hoping for a useful legacy or inheritance, are sometimes alarmed at the prospect of the old person's assets being devoured by care fees. The old person herself (less commonly himself, since a sexist mother nature is not even-handed in such matters) may be keen to ensure that something is handed down. And there may well

---

1 2000 SCLR 163 *affd* 2000 SLT (Sh Ct) 67.
2 At one stage it was argued that the application fell within s 8(1)(b). And certainly there is little difference, on this point, between the present facts and the facts of *Bank of Ireland* v *Bass Brewers Ltd* (above), a s 8(1)(b) case—other than the fact that the document in question (the variation of a standard security) was bilateral in form.
3 It may be noted, however, that the sheriff principal (C G B Nicholson) was a Law Commissioner at the time when the Scottish Law Commission produced its *Report on Rectification of Contractual and Other Documents* (Scot Law Com No 79, 1983) on which the rectification provisions are based.
4 2000 SC 515, 2000 SLT 819.

be a feeling that the state *should* provide the necessary care, free of charge. And so an idea is conceived. Why not donate the capital assets to the next generation, or even to the one after that? In practice, that often means the house. Granny can carry on living there until she has to go into care. But the more attractive this arrangement is to the family, the less it is to the local authority, on which the burden will fall. Local authorities are increasingly looking for ways for fighting back, and there are some legislative provisions in their favour.

It is the *Yule* case which has been providing the headlines, and another, and probably final, instalment, happened in 2000.[1] Rhoda Yule was owner of 195A Stonelaw Road, Rutherglen. In March 1995, when she was 78 years old, she disponed it to her granddaughter, Deborah Yule, reserving to herself a liferent. The disposition was gratuitous. The house was Rhoda Yule's only significant capital asset. In June 1996 she had to go to a nursing home.

Section 12 of the Social Work (Scotland) Act 1968, as amended, imposes on local authorities a duty to provide residential accommodation in certain cases. The financial consequences are dealt with by s 22 of the National Assistance Act 1948—the very name takes one back to another era—which provides that where a person in care cannot pay the full cost, the local authority shall make an assessment to determine how much he or she can pay. The balance is met by the local authority. Detailed provisions are made by statutory instrument. The National Assistance (Assessment of Resources) Regulations 1992[2] provide that the first £16,000 of capital falls to be disregarded. That wee nest-egg can be preserved for the family. But any capital over and above that is deemed available to pay for care fees.[3] Regulation 25 provides that if the person has alienated an asset for the purpose of avoiding liability for fees then that person can be assessed as if he or she still had that asset.[4]

Mrs Yule's local authority found out about the disposition by Mrs Yule to her granddaughter. They took the view that there had been an intentional deprivation of assets. Accordingly, their assessment included the value of the house that Mrs Yule had donated to her granddaughter. Mrs Yule, acting through her son David Yule (who held a power of attorney), sought to reduce the assessment. He failed in the Outer House[5] but reclaimed. The Inner House has now also ruled in favour of the local authority.

The issue in the appeal was whether the local authority had acted reasonably. Mr Yule argued that the approach of the local authority was effectively to throw the burden of proof on the family. The court did not agree:

---

1 *Yule v South Lanarkshire Council* 2000 SLT 1249, 2001 SCLR 26. For a valuable study see W Neilson 2000 SLT (News) 330 and the same author's book, *Residential Care Fees: Defend the Assets!* (2000).

2 SI 1992/2977.

3 Regulation 20: 'No resident shall be assessed as unable to pay for his accommodation at the standard rate if his capital calculated in accordance with regulation 21 exceeds £16,000.'

4 'A resident may be treated as possessing actual capital of which he has deprived himself for the purpose of decreasing the amount that he may be liable to pay for his accommodation.'

5 1998 SLT 490, 1999 SCLR 985.

> The local authority cannot look into the mind of the person making the disposition of capital or of others who may be concerned in the transaction. It can only look at the nature of the disposal within the context of the time at which and the circumstances in which that disposal took place.[1]

The determination of the local authority had not been unreasonable and therefore the challenge failed.

One of the arguments which Mr Yule ran in the Outer House was that s 21 of the Health and Social Services Adjudication Act 1983 has a similar provision but limited to disposals within the previous six months. It was held that the local authority had been correct in invoking the provisions mentioned above, which have no time limit. No appeal was made on this issue.

Another very similar case in 2000 was *Robertson* v *Fife Council*.[2] Mary Robertson owned 87 Main Street, Newmills, Fife. In 1995 she gratuitously disponed it to her children Alexander, Graham and Gavin. She continued to live there until 1998 when she had to go into a nursing home. The local authority was asked to assume responsibility for the fees. They carried out an assessment, and decided that her capital assets were to be deemed to be over the threshold of £16,000. The reason was that the Council considered that the 1995 disposition was a voluntary disposal of assets for the purpose of avoiding liability for fees. Gavin Robertson, acting under power of attorney, sought to reduce the local authority's determination. He averred specific reasons why the disposition had been granted, being reasons unconnected to the possibility of liability for care fees. His action was unsuccessful. Lady Cosgrove remarked that:[3]

> The reality of the situation is that in seeking to operate reg 25, local authorities are likely to meet with denials that the purpose of a transfer of a capital asset of an elderly person was to decrease the amount that he or she might be likely to pay for accommodation under the Social Work (Scotland) Act 1968. There is no power to compel the provision of information, and in such circumstances the local authority must determine the true purpose of any transfer from the information which has been provided to it.

It may be wondered whether such victories by local authorities are not, at the end of the day, pyrrhic. It is one thing to determine that the elderly person must pay: it is another to make her pay. It is all very well saying that the value of the house falls to be included in the notional assets, but that does not imply that the house can be sold to satisfy the charges. Where the transfer is made within six months before the person 'begins to reside' in the special accommodation, the transferee can be made directly liable to the local

---

1 2000 SLT 1249 at 1257E.
2 2000 SLT 1226.
3 At p 1232J.

authority.[1] But in practice the transfer has usually been made more than six months previously.

The local authority could always sequestrate the elderly person and then try to challenge the transfer as a gratuitous alienation. So far as we know, no local authority has yet gone down this road. A gratuitous alienation is not challengeable unless, at the time it was made, the granter was insolvent, or was made insolvent by the transfer. In practice, it seems unlikely that a challenge would be successful, at least in the typical case.

It may be that the elderly person does have some other capital. For example, suppose that she has a house worth £150,000 and savings worth £16,000, and she transfers the house one year before going into care. If the house can be notionally included in her capital assets, that opens the door to recovery against the £16,000, which would otherwise have been exempt. And if she is in an independent care home, the local authority may be able simply to refuse to meet the costs, thereby handing the problem over to the care home and the family.

Finally, in late 2000 and early 2001 the question of care for the elderly was making headline news, and in January 2001 came close to splitting the ruling coalition. The question was whether the recommendations of the Sutherland Commission[2] should be implemented. Whilst legislation is probable, the final form of such legislation remains, as we go to press, uncertain.

ABOLITION OF FEUDAL TENURE ETC (SCOTLAND) ACT 2000

Timetable

The Abolition of Feudal Tenure etc (Scotland) Act 2000 (asp 5) received Royal Assent on 9 June 2000. Currently, very little of the Act is in force. The idea is that it should come into force in three distinct stages, thus:

Phase 1: 9 June 2000

- Restriction of long leases to 175 years.
- Abolition of feudal irritancy.
- Revised rules for descriptions in standard securities.

Phase 2: June 2002?

- Part 4 of the 2000 Act, which provides for the registration of notices to save certain classes of feudal burdens, or to preserve a right to compensation for the extinction of such burdens.

---

1   Health and Social Services and Social Security Adjudication Act 1983, s 21.
2   *Report of the Royal Commission on Long Term Care* (1999, Cm 4192, ISBN 0 101 41922 8). This was chaired by Edinburgh University Principal, Sir Stewart Sutherland.

Phase 3: Martinmas 2003? Whitsunday 2004?

- The rest of the Act. The Act refers to the day when Phase 3 comes into force as the 'appointed day'. The appointed day is the day when the feudal system dies. It is likely that the Title Conditions (Scotland) Bill will come into force on the same day.[1]

At present it is not possible to be definite about the timetable of the later phases. For both Phase 2 and Phase 3 the relevant provisions of the Act are to be brought into force by order, and in both cases six months must elapse between the date of the order and the commencement date.[2] So there will be reasonable notice. The appointed day (*ie* the day of feudal abolition) must be one of the term days (*ie* Whitsunday or Martinmas), for ease of dealing with feuduty. Probably Phase 2 will not begin until the Title Conditions Bill has received Royal Assent. A draft of that Bill was published by the Scottish Law Commission in October 2000[3] and, following consultation, is expected to be introduced to the Scottish Parliament towards the end of 2001. That might suggest Royal Assent around June 2002. So an informed guess would be that Phase 2 will not begin before June 2002. Phase 2 itself has to last a reasonable time to give an opportunity to register notices preserving real burdens. It seems doubtful if it could be less than a year, and it might well be longer. If that is right, the appointed day—the actual day of feudal abolition—will not be until 2003 or even 2004.

A full explanation of the thinking behind the Act will be found in the Scottish Law Commission's *Report on Abolition of the Feudal System*.[4] Both the text of the Act, with explanatory notes,[5] and the Parliamentary debates, are available on the internet.[6] The Bill was debated by the full Parliament on 15 December 1999 (cols 1542–1588) and on 3 May 2000 (cols 214–267). It was considered in Committee by the Justice and Home Affairs Committee on 15 March 2000 (cols 915–961), 21 March 2000 (cols 969–1002), and 29 March 2000 (cols 1008–1030).

The 2000 Act is best understood by beginning at the end, with feudal abolition itself, and then working backwards through the earlier phases. The first topic to be considered, therefore, is Phase 3.

The end of feudalism (Phase 3)

The bulk of the Abolition & Feudal Tenure etc (Scotland) Act 2000 comes into force on a day yet to be fixed but referred to throughout the Act as the 'appointed day'.[7] The appointed day will be a term day, and is unlikely to be before 2003.

---

1 It is so provided by ss 113(1) (definition of 'appointed day') and 119(2) of that Bill.
2 Abolition of Feudal Tenure etc (Scotland) Act 2000, ss 71 and 77(2), (4).
3 See Scottish Law Commission, *Report on Real Burdens* (Scot Law Com No 181), available at www.scotlaw.gov.uk, as discussed above at pp 75–80.
4 Scot Law Com No 168 (February 1999). This can be accessed at www.scotland.gov.uk/library/documents-w10/afs1–01.htm
5 www.scotland-legislation.hmso.gov.uk/legislation/scotland/acts2000/20000005.htm
6 www.scottish.parliament.uk/official_report/meeting.html
7 Defined in s 71.

On the appointed day:

- the feudal system will be abolished
- all existing feuduties will be extinguished
- all rights of superiors to enforce real burdens will fall
- miscellaneous other changes will occur.

These four events are considered in turn.

Feudal abolition

The scene is set by the opening provisions of the Act. Section 1 provides that:

> The feudal system of land tenure, that is to say the entire system whereby land is held by a vassal on perpetual tenure from a superior is, on the appointed day, abolished.

Section 2 then sets out the three main consequences of feudal abolition. First, *dominium utile* is to become full *dominium*—*ie* outright (or simple) ownership. Thus:

> (1) An estate of *dominium utile* of land shall, on the appointed day, cease to exist as a feudal estate but shall forthwith become the ownership of the land and, in so far as is consistent with the provisions of this Act, the land shall be subject to the same subordinate real rights and other encumbrances as was the estate of *dominium utile*.

Second, all superiorities are extinguished:

> (2) Every other feudal estate in land shall, on that day, cease to exist.

That includes the paramount superiority of the Crown. However, it is made clear by s 58 that Crown rights deriving from the royal prerogative are not affected, and this is expressly said to include rights arising under the *regalia majora*—rights held by the Crown on behalf of the public, such as the public right of navigation, or the right of use of the foreshore. This was a matter of some controversy during the progress of the Bill through Parliament.

Finally, no new feudalism can arise:

> (3) It shall, on that day, cease to be possible to create a feudal estate in land.

Nor is feudalism to be possible by the back door through the use of long leases. By s 67 leases are limited in duration to 175 years.[1]

The same rules are to apply to the Kindly Tenants of Lochmaben. On the appointed day all Kindly Tenancies are converted into ownership.[2]

Extinction of feuduty

The provisions on feuduty are set out in Part 2 of the Act. Most feuduty has, of course, already been redeemed under ss 4 to 6 of the Land Tenure Reform

---

1 See below for details.
2 Abolition of Feudal Tenure etc (Scotland) Act 2000, s 64.

(Scotland) Act 1974. But an unallocated *cumulo* cannot be redeemed under the 1974 Act provisions, and most feuduties which remain probably come into this category. All will now fall on the appointed day.[1] No action need be taken by either superior or vassal. The extinction is automatic.

The former superior is, however, entitled to compensation (a 'compensatory payment'), calculated on the usual basis, *ie* by reference to the price of two and a half per cent Consolidated Stock on the day before the appointed day.[2] So the price on that day will fix the amount payable, no matter when compensation is asked for. The compensation payable is then calculated by multiplying the annual feuduty by the feuduty factor. Any unpaid arrears will also have to be paid.[3] Naturally, no feuduty will be due for any period after the appointed day.[4]

The 1974 Act required the vassal to seek out the superior. The Abolition of Feudal Tenure etc (Scotland) Act 2000 requires the superior to seek out the vassal. Feuduty itself is extinguished automatically, and compensation is due only if the superior claims it. The method by which he must do so is laid down in ss 8 to 11 of the Act. A notice must be served on the former vassal, during the two years immediately following the appointed day.[5] Note that this may not be done before the appointed day. Two forms of notice are set out in the schedules to the Act, one for *cumulo* feuduties and one for allocated feuduties.[6] In the case of a *cumulo* feuduty it is for the (former) superior to allocate the compensation figure among the (former) vassals, but he is directed to use any existing apportionments, where such exist.[7] Unless the compensation is less than £50, the form must be accompanied by an instalment document, as set out in Schedule 3.[8]

The former vassal can pay at once. Or he can opt to pay in instalments (unless the amount due is less than £50). To pay by instalments he must complete and return the instalment document within eight weeks, with payment of one-tenth of the total compensation.[9] This is an extra sum, in place of interest. Instalments must be paid half yearly at Whitsunday and Martinmas. The number of instalments depends on the amount of compensation. The maximum number allowed is 20, for compensation of more that £1,500.[10] So payment could linger on for up to 10 years after feudal abolition.

A key change is that feuduty is severed from the land. Compensation is merely a personal debt due by the person who happened to be vassal just before feudal abolition. A person who buys the property the following day has no liability. The same is true of any arrears of feuduty.[11] This means that, from the appointed day, purchasers no longer have to concern themselves with the

---

1 2000 Act, s 7.
2 2000 Act, s 9(1).
3 2000 Act, s 13(1).
4 2000 Act, s 7.
5 2000 Act, s 7(1).
6 Schedules 1 and 2 respectively.
7 2000 Act, s 9(4).
8 2000 Act, s 10(1).
9 2000 Act, s 10(2).
10 2000 Act, s 10(4).
11 2000 Act, s 13(2), (3).

feuduty position. An incoming owner cannot be made to pay. Indeed, it is the seller who is likely to want to keep the feuduty redemption receipt, in case a claim is made against him by the former superior.

As with the 1974 Act, identical rules are applied to other periodical payments—ground annual, skat, standard charge, and the like.[1]

Extinction of superiors' rights to enforce real burdens

Section 17(1) provides that:

(1) Subject to sections 18, 19, 20, 23, 27, 28 and 60 of this Act—

    (a) a real burden which, immediately before the appointed day, is enforceable by, and only by, a superior shall on that day be extinguished; and

    (b) any other real burden shall, on and after that day, not be enforceable by a former superior

With the fall of the feudal system there fall also all rights of superiors (by now, former superiors) to enforce real burdens—at any rate in their capacity as superiors. The effect on the real burdens in question depends on whether

- *only* the superior could enforce, or
- the burdens were also enforceable by neighbours (*ie* co-feuars).

The different consequences here are spelled out in s 17(1). If only a superior could enforce, the burdens fall. If others could also enforce, their rights are undisturbed and the burdens remain. In practice it will often not be easy to determine which burdens fall into which category. Sometimes of course co-feuars are given express rights of enforcement. In that case the position is generally clear.[2] But if the feudal grant is silent, the position is determined by application of the rules on implied enforcement rights. Under the present law these rules are so complex as to be almost unworkable.[3] Fortunately, they are to be reformed and simplified by the Title Conditions Bill, which, it is intended, will also come into force on the appointed day.[4]

All this will take some time to work out. For the time being real burdens will stay on the Land Register even if they have been extinguished by s 17. In due course, owners will be able to apply to the Keeper for removal of the burdens (by means of the rectification procedure). But s 46(1) prevents any application from being brought until such date as may be fixed by statutory instrument. That date is likely to be several years after feudal abolition. It is envisaged that the initiative for deletion of burdens will come from owners—possibly under the stimulus of a prospective sale. Given the vast number of title sheets, it would be impracticable for the Keeper to undertake this work on his own.

---

1 2000 Act, s 56.
2 Although note that the existence of express enforcement rights does not, of itself, exclude enforcement rights arising by implication. See Scottish Law Commission, *Report on Real Burdens* (Scot Law Com No 181) para 11.2.
3 Scottish Law Commission, *Report on Real Burdens* (Scot Law Com No 181) paras 11.1 to 11.27.
4 See Part 4 of the Title Conditions (Scotland) Bill, summarised earlier in this volume.

The opening words of s 17(1) will be noted. The sections listed are exceptions to the extinction of feudal real burdens. These exceptions are discussed below.

It is worth stressing that the Act has no effect on *non-feudal* real burdens, *ie* burdens created in a disposition, or in a deed of conditions granted in association with dispositions. Only burdens created in feudal grants are affected—perhaps one-half of all burdens. The Title Conditions Bill, however, will apply to all real burdens, however created. It might be added that the 2000 Act has no effect on servitudes.

Other miscellaneous changes

A number of other changes in the law will occur on the appointed day. The following are among the more important:

Abolition of warrants of registration.[1] Already, of course, warrants are not required for the Land Register. Now they will be dispensed with for Sasine conveyancing also. But it will continue to be necessary to complete an application form.[2]

Abolition of entails (tailzies).[3] There cannot be many left.

Abolition of thirlage (*ie* the obligation to take corn to a particular mill).[4] Thirlage has long since disappeared but was never formally abolished.

Severance of the dignity of baron (ie *the right to the name) from the land.*[5] Dignities will now become free-floating (incorporeal) rights, transferable by assignation and without registration. For the purposes of land law, barony titles—with their peculiar and obscure 'privileges'[6]—will disappear entirely.

It is also made clear that *a partnership can own land in its own name.*[7] The current position is that it is prevented from doing so by the feudal system. But this is unlikely to lead to a change in the present practice by which title is taken in the name of trustees for behoof of the partnership. This is because, as the law currently stands, partnerships can dissolve easily and unexpectedly, and so are unsuitable for long-term ownership. It may be noted that the position here may change as a result of reform proposals currently being prepared by the Scottish Law Commission and the Law Commission of England and Wales.[8]

---

1 Abolition of Feudal Tenure etc (Scotland) Act 2000, s 5.
2 The form is now put on a statutory basis: see s 5(2).
3 2000 Act, ss 50–52.
4 2000 Act, s 55.
5 2000 Act, s 63.
6 For which see Scottish Law Commission, *Report on Abolition of the Feudal System* (Scot Law Com No 168) para 2.39.
7 2000 Act, s 70.
8 *Partnership: A Joint Consultation Paper* (Scot Law Com DP No 111, 2000), available on www.scotlawcom.gov.uk

Saving real burdens (Phase 2)

As already explained, all superiors' rights to enforce real burdens are extinguished on the appointed day.[1] In turn this will often lead to the extinction of the real burden itself because, with the superior gone, there will be no one left to enforce it. But to these principles, the Act introduces a number of exceptions. The idea is to allow the preservation of burdens that are obviously meritorious, for otherwise feudal abolition would leave a vacuum in the private regulation of land which would hardly be acceptable.

Classification of burdens

The easiest way to understand the exceptions is to divide real burdens into two broad categories. In the first place there are burdens which are concerned with the maintenance and management of facilities. These may be termed 'facility burdens'. The Act gives (non-exhaustive) examples of such facilities:[2]

a common part of a tenement building;
a common area for recreation;
a private road;
private sewerage;
a boundary wall.

Most facility burdens will be concerned with common maintenance, for example of the roof of a tenement, or of a shared garden; and almost always the 'facility' will be shared by more than one property.

The other broad category comprises 'amenity burdens', that is to say, burdens imposed on one property in order to preserve the amenity of neighbouring property or properties. By contrast with facility burdens, amenity burdens are almost always negative in character.[3] They *stop* the owner doing something, such as building, or carrying on a business.

The terms 'facility burden' and 'amenity burden' are not used in the Act, but they are useful labels none the less.[4] The two types of burden are treated by the Act in quite different ways.

Facility burdens

Facility burdens survive feudal abolition. Section 23 provides that a feudal burden which qualifies as a facility burden will not be extinguished on the appointed day. Instead, it will in future be enforceable by the owners[5] of those

---

1 2000 Act, s 17(1).
2 2000 Act, s 24(4).
3 For the distinction between 'negative' burdens and 'affirmative' burdens, see Scottish Law Commission, *Report on Real Burdens* (Scot Law Com No 181) paras 2.1 to 2.3.
4 The term 'facility burdens' is however used in the Title Conditions Bill. For the different methods of classifying real burdens, see Scottish Law Commission, *Report on Real Burdens* (Scot Law Com No 181) para 1.9 and n 23.
5 Note that, in its current form, the Title Conditions Bill (s 7(2)) will extend enforcement rights to tenants and other holders of possessory real rights.

properties which take benefit from the facility. In effect, interest to enforce determines title to enforce.[1] Such an owner may—or may not—include the former superior. In order to qualify the former superior would have to own neighbouring land which benefited from the facility. Section 23 effects an automatic saving—in other words, no action is required by anyone. This contrasts with the rule for amenity burdens (discussed below).

An example shows how s 23 will work. Take the case of a small housing estate comprising 30 houses. Suppose that the estate was feued out in the 1960s. The estate has some recreational ground and a private lane. The deed of conditions provides that each house is to contribute equally to the maintenance of these facilities. As the law currently stands, the maintenance obligation is enforceable by the superiors (builders). It may, or may not, also be enforceable by the owners against one another. That depends on how the deed is worded. Assume that it is not so enforceable. On the appointed day the right to enforce the burdens will pass from the superiors to the individual owners. The superiors will lose their rights unless they happen to own one of the houses.

Most cases should be as straightforward as the one just described. Inevitably, however, there will be marginal cases where it seems less clear whether the thing being maintained is a 'facility', and, if so, which properties take benefit from it.

There is one exception. Victorian charters frequently impose obligations in relation to, *eg*, roads and sewers which have later been taken over by the local authority. Real burdens falling into this category are expressly excluded, and will be formally extinguished on the appointed day.[2]

Amenity burdens

In relation to facility burdens a (former) superior will retain enforcement rights only if he owns property in the neighbourhood which takes benefit from the facility. Much the same principle is applied by the Act to amenity burdens. But here there is no general distribution of enforcement rights. A neighbour without enforcement rights today will not receive such rights as a result of the Act. With amenity burdens the policy is to avoid proliferation of enforcement rights. For otherwise it would be impossible for the burdened owner ever to get a minute of waiver. It would be an ironic consequence of feudal abolition if the single superior were to be replaced by 20 neighbours. As it is, all attention is focused on the superior. At present the superior has enforcement rights. On the appointed day, he will lose them.[3] But s 18 allows the superior to preserve enforcement rights, in certain circumstances, if he owns neighbouring land.[4] The idea is that,

---

1 Section 23 is repealed by the Title Conditions Bill and replaced by s 47 of that Bill. But in all important respects the terms of s 47 are identical. The reason for the replacement is that s 47 applies also to non-feudal burdens.
2 Abolition of Feudal Tenure etc (Scotland) Act 2000, s 23(3).
3 2000 Act, s 17(1).
4 See generally Scottish Law Commission, *Report on Abolition of the Feudal System* (Scot Law Com No 168) paras 4.26 to 4.47.

on the appointed day, the right to enforce the burden passes from the superiority interest to the neighbouring land. The neighbouring land is thus the new benefited property[1] in the real burden. The Act talks of the 'reallotment' of burdens. Once a burden is reallotted to neighbouring land, it remains there for the future. So the burden continues to be enforceable by any successors of the former superior, as owner of that land. In effect feudal burdens are being converted into non-feudal burdens.

Reallotment could not happen automatically. For there would then be no means of knowing, in the future, what land (if any) the former superior had happened to own on the eve of feudal abolition. A selective saving is bound to involve registration. The rules are set out in s 18. The former superior must execute and register a notice, following the form set out in the Act.[2] The notice describes the burden(s), the burdened property (*ie* the feu), and the proposed new benefited property. It must be registered against *both* properties (and not merely, as is usual with real burdens, against the burdened property only). This is the beginning of a change—which is carried much further by the Title Conditions Bill[3]—by which the creation of burdens is to involve dual registration. If one of the properties is in the Land Register and the other in the Register of Sasines, it will be necessary to register in both registers. No warrant of registration is required.[4] Before registration there must be notification to the owner of the burdened property (*ie* to the vassal).[5]

The preconditions for the registration of a notice are quite stringent. There are four preconditions.

In the first place, the title to the land to which the real burden is to be reallotted must match the title to the superiority. Thus, if the land is owned by the 12th Duke and the superiority by the trustees of the 10th Duke, the condition is not satisfied and some preliminary conveyancing will have to be undertaken before reallotment can proceed.[6] Infeftment is not, however, required. Further, the condition need be met only at the time of registration, and there is no objection if the superior subsequently sells the land, even if this is done before the appointed day.

In the second place, there must, in the normal case[7] be situated on the land a permanent building which is in use wholly or mainly as a place of 'human habitation or resort'.[8] So open fields would not do, nor, say, a barn. A typical building for 'human habitation or resort' is a house or a pub or a factory. The underlying policy is that loss of amenity is mainly of relevance in cases involving such buildings.

---

1 Here we use the modern terminology introduced by the Title Conditions Bill. A benefited property is referred to in the 2000 Act as a 'dominant tenement'.
2 In Sched 5.
3 See in particular s 4(5) of the Title Conditions Bill.
4 2000 Act, s 41(2).
5 2000 Act, s 41(3).
6 2000 Act, s 18(1).
7 But see below for some minor exceptions.
8 2000 Act, s 18(7)(a).

In the third place, the building (as opposed to the land itself) must lie within 100 metres of the burdened property (*ie* the feu).[1] This limitation seems created mainly with rural areas in mind.[2]

In the fourth place, the notice must be registered during Phase 2, *ie* in the period beginning with the commencement of the relevant sections and ending with the appointed day.[3] Earlier it was suggested that this might be the period between, say, June 2002 and November 2003. It seems unlikely that the period would be shorter than a year. Registration must take place during this period. Late registration will not be accepted.[4]

There is no formal requirement that the burden be an amenity burden. In theory the procedure could be used for any burden. But since facility burdens are automatically saved, it would be pointless using the procedure for those. The procedure might possibly be used for one or two of the other burdens mentioned below.

If the conditions outlined above cannot be met, it will normally be impossible to preserve an amenity burden. But the Lands Tribunal is empowered, on application, to waive the second and/or third condition. It may do so only where the superior has tried, but failed, to reach agreement with the vassal,[5] and where the Tribunal is satisfied that the extinction of the burden would lead to substantial loss or damage to the superior in his capacity as owner of neighbouring land.[6] The application to the Tribunal must be made during Phase 2, and indeed there is power to shorten this period by statutory instrument.[7]

Other burdens

Not all burdens are facility burdens or amenity burdens. Brief mention will be made here of the remaining categories of real burden provided for by the Act.

Rights of pre-emption and redemption

Like amenity burdens, these may be saved by registration of a notice under s 18, but unlike amenity burdens, there is no requirement that the proposed benefited property contain a building within 100 metres.[8]

---

1 2000 Act, s 18(7)(a).
2 If only because it will be unusual for superiors to own neighbouring land in towns and cities. This means that s 18 is likely to be used mainly for rural properties.
3 2000 Act, s 18(1).
4 Except in the highly unusual case of registration having been refused, and the refusal successfully challenged in the Lands Tribunal. See s 45.
5 2000 Act, s 20(1). Reallotment by agreement is provided for by s 19. These provisions were not part of the bill as published by the Scottish Law Commission.
6 2000 Act, s 20(7). The 'substantial loss or disadvantage' test is one of two alternative tests provided, in s 1(4) of the Conveyancing and Feudal Reform (Scotland) Act 1970, for the awarding of compensation by the Tribunal following variation or discharge. The other test (reduction in original price paid) is used by s 37(2) of the 2000 Act in the context of compensation (discussed below).
7 2000 Act, s 20(1).
8 2000 Act, s 18(7)(b)(ii).

Other cases where 100-metres rule dispensed with

Section 18 notices may also be used, without complying with the 100-metres rule:

- for real burdens (very unusual in practice) which comprise a right to enter or otherwise make use of the burdened property;[1]
- for real burdens created for the benefit of minerals (in which case the mineral estate will be the benefited property);[2] and
- for real burdens created for the benefit of a right of salmon fishing (in which case the salmon fishings will be the benefited property).[3]

So far as minerals are concerned, it is important to note that conditions included in reservations of minerals (*eg* in relation to compensation, or the right to enter or lower the surface) are not usually real burdens nor indeed feudal.[4] They are not feudal because, when a superior reserves the minerals, the effect is to create two estates of *dominium utile*—one for the land being feued and the other for the minerals being retained. The relationship between the estates is not a feudal one. On the appointed day the *dominium utile* of the minerals, like the *dominium utile* of the land, will be converted into full ownership.

Service burdens

A 'service burden' binds the owner of the feu to provide services to other land— for example the supply of water or electricity.[5] Service burdens are rare in practice. The 2000 Act treats them in the same way as facility burdens, that is to say, they survive feudal abolition, after which they are to be enforceable by the owner of the land which receives the service. No action is required by the superior.

Conservation burdens

Section 26 empowers the Scottish Ministers to draw up a list of 'conservation bodies'.[6] A body included on the list, and which is also a feudal superior, can preserve any feudal burdens which it is currently entitled to enforce, provided that the burdens themselves qualify as conservation burdens. Conservation burdens are defined as:[7]

---

1   2000 Act, s 18(7)(b)(i). Section 77 of the Title Conditions (Scotland) Bill provides that such burdens are then converted into positive servitudes on the appointed day.
2   2000 Act, s 18(7)(c)(i).
3   2000 Act, s 18(7)(c)(ii).
4   Scottish Law Commission, *Report on Abolition of the Feudal System* (Scot Law Com No 168) para 6.5.
5   2000 Act, s 23(2). The term 'service burden' does not appear in the 2000 Act, but it is used in s 47 of the Title Conditions (Scotland) Bill, which is to replace s 23 of the 2000 Act.
6   For a discussion, see Scottish Law Commission, *Report on Abolition of the Feudal System* (Scot Law Com No 168) paras 4.52 to 4.61.
7   2000 Act, s 27(2). It should be noted that a number of the provisions on conservation burdens (s 26 and ss 29 to 32) are repealed by the Title Conditions (Scotland) Bill and replaced by Part 3 of that Bill, which makes general provision as to conservation (and maritime) burden, and allows the creation of such burdens in the future.

those real burdens which are enforceable against a feudal estate of *dominium utile* of land for the purpose of preserving, or protecting—

(a) the architectural or historical characteristics of the land; or
(b) any other special characteristics of the land (including, without prejudice to the generality of this paragraph, a special characteristic derived from the flora, fauna or general appearance of the land).

It will be seen that conservation burdens may be concerned both with the natural and with the built environment.

A superior which is a conservation body can preserve conservation burdens by registration of a notice.[1] The Scottish Ministers have the same rights. A statutory form is provided.[2] The notice must be registered during Phase 2— which means before the appointed day. On the appointed day the burdens in question are then converted from feudal burdens into conservation burdens.[3] One oddity of conservation burdens is that there is no benefited property—or in other words, the burdens are held directly by the conservation body, without reference to its ownership of any particular property. In the future the right to a conservation burden will be transferred by registered assignation—but only in favour of another conservation body (or the Scottish Ministers).[4]

Maritime burdens

For completeness, brief mention may be made of maritime burdens. Real burdens affecting the sea bed or foreshore in favour of the Crown as superior are automatically saved by the Act.[5] On the appointed day they are converted from feudal burdens into maritime burdens. No notice is required. Like conservation burdens, a maritime burden is held directly by a person—in this case the Crown—without reference to a benefited property. A maritime burden may not be assigned.

Compensation: development value burdens

If the superior owns land close by, he can generally preserve his real burdens. In the case of facility burdens, this happens automatically, by force of law. In the case of amenity burdens, this requires the registration of a notice under s 18.

Conversely, if the superior does not own land close by, then, arguably, he has no interest to enforce. On that basis he loses nothing on feudal abolition —other than the possibility of extracting payment for minutes of waiver. Consistent with this analysis, the Act does not in general provide for payment of compensation for loss of real burdens.[6] There is one exception.

---

1 2000 Act, s 27.
2 In Sched 8.
3 2000 Act, s 28.
4 2000 Act, s 29.
5 2000 Act, s 60.
6 By contrast, full compensation is given for loss of feuduty (discussed earlier).

The Act recognises a special category of feudal burden, which it labels 'development value burdens'.[1] A development value burden is one which, in feuing land, reserves to the superior the development value.[2] 'Development value' is defined as:[3]

> any significant increase in the value of the land arising as a result of the land becoming free to be used, or dealt with, in some way not permitted under the grant in feu.

Like other feudal burdens, a development value burden will be extinguished on the appointed day (unless it can be saved under one of the heads set out above). But compensation may be available if either no consideration was paid for the original grant in feu, or if the consideration was 'significantly' lower on account of the burden.[4] An obvious example would be a gift of land subject to the condition that it was to be used only for some stipulated purpose such as a village hall or a sports field.

Compensation under the Act works as follows. For the first 20 years after the appointed day, burdens falling into this category can be made to live on in a shadow form. Such a burden cannot be enforced directly (because it has been extinguished); but if it is 'breached' during this period the former superior is entitled to compensation. Some method is required of distinguishing the burdens in question from other feudal burdens, for warning a future owner that compensation might be claimed, and for identifying the potential claimant. The Act achieves this by requiring the registration of an appropriate notice.[5] As usual this must be done during Phase 2, ie before the appointed day. If no notice is registered by then, no compensation can become due.

In practice a relatively small number of burdens are likely to qualify for compensation under this head, for a number of reasons.

First, as already mentioned, a notice can be registered only where there was no consideration for the feu, or the consideration was significantly lower on account of the burden. This excludes altogether the standard package of real burdens.[6] Only an unusual burden or set of burdens would have that effect. In completing a notice the superior is required to put an actual figure on the reduction in consideration.[7] To qualify, the reduction must be 'significant'.

Second, conditions which seek to reserve development value are quite often not valid real burdens at all. That is almost certainly the case if the condition merely provides for a cash payment (whether quantified or not) in the event

1 See generally Scottish Law Commission, *Report on Abolition of the Feudal System* (Scot Law Com No 168) paras 5.14 to 5.57.
2 2000 Act, s 33(1)(a).
3 2000 Act, s 33(5).
4 2000 Act, s 33(1)(b).
5 2000 Act, s 33.
6 It probably excludes most cases of commercial clawback. If land is sold on the basis that the seller is to have a share in the uplift in value in the event that planning consent is granted, the price paid at the time of sale is usually the current market value of the property. In that case, there is no 'significant' reduction in price consequent on the real burdens (which, by restricting use to current purposes, may give the seller a lever to obtain a share in the uplift).
7 2000 Act, s 33(2)(e).

that the land is used for a particular purpose. This is because a bare obligation to pay money is not 'praedial', *ie* is not connected with the *dominium directum* reserved by the superior.[1] If a condition is not a valid real burden, then of course there can be no question of compensation.

Finally, no compensation may be payable if development value can be recovered in some other way.[2] In modern practice, at least, an alternative means of recovery would often be available—for example, by means of a standard security, or a clause of redemption.

Assuming (i) that a notice is duly registered and (ii) that the shadow burden is duly breached in the 20 years following the appointed day (or the five years before), then (iii) the former superior is entitled to compensation.[3] He must make a formal claim, within three years.[4] In principle he is then entitled to the increase in development value caused by the notional freeing of the burden which allowed the breach—or in other words, to the difference in the value of land with the burden and its value if the burden had been modified to the extent of the breach.[5] But this is subject to a cap: however many claims are made, the total compensation paid cannot exceed 'such sum as will make up for any effect which the burden produced, at the time when it was imposed, in reducing the consideration then paid or made payable for the feu'.[6] This is the formula already familiar from awards of compensation made by the Lands Tribunal following variation or discharge of a burden.[7] The Tribunal has jurisdiction to determine compensation in the event of a dispute.[8]

Implications for current practice

Although the appointed day remains some time away, the 2000 Act has a number of implications for current practice.

To feu or not to feu?

An obvious question is whether there is any point in continuing to feu. In general, the answer must be 'no'. A superiority interest reserved today will last only for another three years or so. It is not really worth bothering about. Further, it deflects attention from the real issue, which is how real burdens are to be imposed in the future. The short answer here is that real burdens can be imposed if and only if there is some land in the neighbourhood which is capable of acting as a benefited property. Assuming that this condition is met, there is no point in feuing.

---

1 Scottish Law Commission, *Report on Abolition of the Feudal System* (Scot Law Com No 168) para 5.23.
2 2000 Act, s 37(3).
3 2000 Act, s 35(1), (2).
4 2000 Act, ss 35(3)–(6), 36.
5 2000 Act, s 37(1).
6 2000 Act, s 37(2).
7 Conveyancing and Feudal Reform (Scotland) Act 1970, s 1(4)(ii). For a discussion of this provision, see Sir Crispin Agnew of Lochnaw, *Variation and Discharge of Land Obligations* (1999) pp 135–138.
8 2000 Act, s 44(2).

In practice, real burdens are likely to be used mainly in two situations. One is where an owner sells part of his land while retaining another part. In that case burdens can be imposed on the part that is sold for the benefit of the part that is retained.[1] The other situation is where a housing estate or other development is being sold. Here the deed of conditions can provide that the burdens are to be reciprocally enforceable, so that each unit is both a burdened property and also a benefited property. Once it is in force, the Title Conditions Bill will require that the benefited property be expressly nominated,[2] but this should always be done even under the present law. For otherwise future enforcement will depend on the difficult and obscure rules on implied enforcement rights.[3] A simple form of words will have the desired result. So for example in the first of the two situations identified earlier, the disposition should declare the burdens to be enforceable 'by me and my successors as owners of [*describe the benefited property*]'.

If no neighbouring land is being retained, it may be worth exploring alternatives, such as a long lease instead of an outright sale. The Act, however, caps new long leases at 175 years.[4]

In some unusual situations there may be something to be said for continuing to feu. Examples might include:

(1) Where the remainder of a development is being sold off and the earlier parts were feued. Feuing here ensures uniformity, for what that is worth.

(2) Where the seller does not own neighbouring land at the moment but expects to do so before the appointed day. In that case the seller could (i) feu imposing real burdens and (ii) once the neighbouring land had been acquired, register a notice under s 18 reallotting the burdens to the neighbouring land. It will be borne in mind that in order to qualify the neighbouring land must usually contain a building within 100 metres of the burdened property (*ie* the feu).

(3) Where the seller is a body of the kind which might be included on the list of conservation bodies. In that case the seller could (i) feu imposing conservation burdens and (ii) if subsequently included on the list of conservation bodies, register a notice under s 27 preserving the right to enforce the burdens.

Advising superiors

Those who act for superiors will have to advise them on the effect of the new legislation, and on what steps will need to be taken in the next year or two. The various notices preserving real burdens (or reserving the right to compensation) will have to be registered during the relatively short period, referred to in this

---

1 The situation is much the same if *both* parts are sold, although in that case it may be desirable to impose burdens on each, for the benefit of the other.

2 Title Conditions (Scotland) Bill, s 4(2)(c). The deed must then be registered against both properties: s 4(5).

3 Described in K G C Reid, *The Law of Property in Scotland* (1996) paras 397–404. Another reason for not relying on the implied rights is that such rights will be substantially swept away by Part 4 of the Title Conditions (Scotland) Bill.

4 2000 Act, s 67, discussed below.

book as Phase 2. Phase 2 is unlikely to begin before the middle of 2002, at earliest, but some forward planning would be helpful, particularly in the case of superiors with a substantial number of feus.

The main issue to consider is likely to be whether it is worth trying to save burdens under s 18. A number of issues arise. Might the burdens be saved anyway, because they are facility or service burdens (under s 23)? If so, no action need be taken. If not, there are further questions. Does the superior own land which could act as the benefited property? Does the land have on it a building for 'human habitation and resort' and within 100 metres of the feu? Are these conditions satisfied for all of the feus or only for some? Should all the burdens be saved or can some be dispensed with?

The trouble—and therefore the cost—involved will have to be weighed against the possible benefits. At this point it is important to bear in mind that the Title Conditions Bill makes it easier to gain release from real burdens. In particular, it introduces a procedure by which real burdens which are more than 100 years old can be extinguished simply by service and registration by the *burdened* owner of a notice of termination.[1] In other words, the burdens could be removed without the consent of the *benefited* owner—although it would be possible for that owner to go to the Lands Tribunal to seek renewal of the burdens. Assuming this procedure forms part of the eventual legislation, there may be little point in preserving burdens which are more than 100 years old—or even those within the range of, say, 80 to 100 years.

It may also be necessary to give advice in relation to conservation burdens, and to the possibility of preserving a right to compensation. But both of these may turn out to be relatively unusual in practice.

As already explained, the compensation due for the extinction of feuduty must be collected in the first two years following the appointed day. It cannot be collected before then. Superiors with significant outstanding feuduty will be well advised to sort out their records, and put in place procedures to claim the compensation at the appropriate time.

Advising vassals

Unlike superiors, vassals—ordinary owners—do not have anything to do. They will be relieved both of real burdens and of feuduty simply by virtue of the Act. Clearly, the potential disappearance of real burdens is a factor to be taken into account if the vassal is considering doing something which is or may be in breach of a burden. So also, doubtless, is the fact that irritancy is no longer available to the superior.[2] In deciding whether a particular burden will disappear on the appointed day, the vassal will have to bear in mind the possibility of enforcement rights being held by neighbours, and of such rights surviving feudal abolition.

---

1 Title Conditions (Scotland) Bill, ss 18 to 22.
2 2000 Act, s 53, discussed below.

Provisions already in force (Phase 1)

Finally, a small number of the provisions of the 2000 Act came into force on 9 June 2000, the day on which the Act received Royal Assent. Only the following are of consequence.

Abolition of irritancy

Section 53 abolishes the right of a superior to irritate the feu, whether for non-payment of feuduty[1] or for failure to comply with real burdens. Any action which was in court on 9 June 2000 falls. No new action may be raised. Naturally, both real burdens and the obligation to pay feuduty can continue to be judicially enforced by other means—interdict, actions for payment, and so on.

Restriction on the length of leases

Residential leases have been restricted to 20 years since 1974.[2] Now s 67 of the 2000 Act restricts all other leases to 175 years.[3] Both the period and the principle were controversial. Some felt that there should be no restriction on the length of leases. Others accepted that a restriction was justified if Scotland was to avoid a second feudal system being created by leasehold titles, on the English model, but felt that the period should be longer than the 125 years recommended by the Scottish Law Commission. As introduced to Parliament, the Bill provided for 125 years, but an amendment was then moved by the Executive to increase this to 175 years.

Section 67 is worth quoting in full:

(1) Notwithstanding any provision to the contrary in any lease, no lease of land executed on or after the coming into force of this section (in this section referred to as the 'commencement date') may continue for a period of more than 175 years; and any such lease which is still subsisting at the end of that period shall, by virtue of this subsection, be terminated forthwith.

(2) If a lease of land so executed includes provision (however expressed) requiring the landlord or the tenant to renew the lease then the duration of any such renewed lease shall be added to the duration of the original lease for the purposes of reckoning the period mentioned in subsection (1) above.

(3) Nothing in subsection (1) above shall prevent—

    (a) any lease being continued by tacit relocation; or

    (b) the duration of any lease being extended by, under or by virtue of any enactment.

---

1 The irritancy *ob non solutem canonem*.
2 Land Tenure Reform (Scotland) Act 1974, ss 8 to 10.
3 See Scottish Law Commission, *Report on Abolition of the Feudal System* (Scot Law Com No 162) paras 9.40 to 9.42.

(4) Subsections (1) and (2) above do not apply—

    (a) to a lease executed on or after the commencement date in implement of an obligation entered into before that date;

    (b) to a lease executed after the commencement date in implement of an obligation contained in a lease such as is mentioned in paragraph (a) above; or

    (c) where—

        (i) a lease for a period of more than 175 years has been executed before the commencement date; or

        (ii) a lease such as is mentioned in paragraph (a) or (b) above is executed on or after that date,

    to a sub-lease executed on or after that date of the whole, or part, of the land subject to the lease in question.

(5) For the purposes of this section 'lease' includes sub-lease.

The main provision is straightforward. Whatever a lease might actually say about duration, it cannot continue for more than 175 years. So if a lease provides for a duration of, say, 150 years, that is fine. The lease then lasts for the full contractual term. But if the stipulated duration is 200 years, s 67(1) will override the contractual term and bring the lease to an end after 175 years.

The limitation applies only to new leases, *ie* to leases executed on or after the day the section came into force—which was 9 June 2000. Since leases are usually bilateral in form, this means executed by *both* parties to the lease. Existing long leases are unaffected, at least for the time being. The whole subject of long leases is, however, currently under consideration by the Scottish Law Commission, which may in due course recommend legislation allowing certain classes of long lease to be converted into ownership.[1]

Section 67(4)(a) contains a transitional provision. The 175-year limitation does not apply to a lease executed after 9 June 2000 if this was in implement of an obligation entered into before that date. That obligation would normally be contained in a contract, but might also be contained in an existing lease (*ie* that lease might contain an option, typically in favour of the tenant, allowing for the renewal of the lease for a further period).

More needs to be said about options to renew. If one party to a lease has an option to renew, this means that the other party has a corresponding obligation to grant the renewal. So if the tenant has an option, the landlord has a corresponding obligation. As a general rule, forced renewals are treated by s 67(2) as part of the original term. So if there is a lease for 99 years with an option in favour of the tenant to renew for another 99, then this is treated as a lease for 198 years. Accordingly, if renewed, the lease comes to an end automatically after 175 years. The idea is to prevent the 175-year limit being avoided by a chain of consecutive leases. The position is different if, at the end

---

1 Scottish Law Commission, *Sixth Programme of Law Reform* (Scot Law Com No 176, 2000) paras 2.11 and 2.12.

of one 99-year lease, the parties *voluntarily* enter into a second lease for 99 years (there being no option stipulated for in the lease). In that case there are two leases and not one.

But even in relation to chains of leases s 67 offers some relief. As was mentioned earlier, the 175-year limit is not applied where there is (i) a lease entered into prior to 9 June 2000 containing an obligation to renew followed by (ii) a second lease, after 9 June 2000, in implement of that option.[1] Here it does not matter if the second lease is for more than 175 years. *A fortiori* it does not matter if the combined duration of the two leases exceeds 175 years.

Section 67(4)(b) extends the exception by allowing *one* further lease. In other words, if (i) a 200-year lease entered into on 5 January 2000 contains an option to renew for, say, 200 years, and (ii) that lease is then renewed on 5 January 2200 by a lease which itself contains an obligation to renew for a further 200 years, then (iii) the second renewal, due on 5 January 2400, is perfectly competent. But no third renewal is allowed. The purpose of this exception is to permit so-called Blairgowrie leases (chains of leases each with a 99-year term) to continue long enough to allow legislation to be brought forward following the work of the Scottish Law Commission, mentioned earlier.[2] Note, however, that the chain must have started prior to 9 June 2000. This means that new chains of leases are not now possible, and cannot be used as a means of avoiding the 175-year limit.[3]

The 175-year limit has no effect on tacit relocation.[4] So if, after the 175-year period has run, neither party has served a notice to quit, the lease will continue from year to year by tacit relocation.

Sub-leases are also subject to the 175-year rule.[5] Indeed, it could hardly be otherwise, for if the head lease lasts for only 175 years, a sub-lease could not have a longer duration. However, in cases where the duration of the head lease exceeds 175 years—usually because it had been granted prior to 9 June 2000— any sub-lease may also exceed 175 years, even if granted today.[6] Any other result would be commercially inconvenient.

Descriptions in standard securities

Note 1 of Schedule 2 to the Conveyancing and Feudal Reform (Scotland) Act 1970, as enacted, provides that:

> The security subjects shall be described by means of a particular description or by reference to a description thereof as in Schedule D to the Conveyancing (Scotland) Act 1924 or as in Schedule (G) to the Titles to Land Consolidation (Scotland) Act 1868.

---

1 2000 Act, s 67(4)(a).
2 See the explanation given by Mr Angus MacKay to the Justice and Home Affairs Committee of the Scottish Parliament on 29 March 2000.
3 2000 Act, s 67(2).
4 2000 Act, s 67(3)(a).
5 2000 Act, s 67(5).
6 2000 Act, s 67(4)(c).

Note 1 applies only to Sasine transactions and first registrations. Once a property is on the Land Register it is both necessary, and also sufficient, to refer to the title number.[1]

In *Beneficial Bank plc v McConnachie*[2] the effect of note 1 was said to be that a particular description (either directly or by reference) was required in all standard securities. A general description would not do. Accordingly, a standard security which described a terraced house only by its postal address ('the Heritable Subjects known as 57 Longdykes Road, Prestonpans, in the County of East Lothian') failed to satisfy the requirements of note 1.

This is an awkward rule, and one which does not apply to other conveyancing deeds, such as dispositions. Of course in most cases, a standard security does in fact contain a particular description, usually by reference. But there is a special difficulty with tenement flats. What counts as a particular description of a flat? An answer, of sorts, was given in *Beneficial Bank*. With an upper flat it is sufficient to give its location within the building (*eg* 'top flat south'). But with a flat on the ground floor it is necessary to stipulate the boundaries. The reason for the difference is not fully explained.

In practice, of course, ground floor flats have tended to be described in exactly the same way as other flats. The effect of *Beneficial Bank*, therefore, was to make a large number of securities over ground floor flats ineffective. And for new securities, it became necessary to give a bounding description, whether in words or by plan.

This decision, criticised at the time,[3] is now superseded. The 2000 Act substitutes, with effect from 9 June 2000, a new version of note 1 which says merely that:[4]

> The security subjects shall be described sufficiently to identify them; but this note is without prejudice to any additional requirement imposed as respects any register.

The effect of this amendment is to readmit general descriptions. The reference to 'any additional requirements imposed as respects any register' is simply to make clear that the Keeper must be satisfied with the sufficiency of the description.[5] But this is no more than the rule that applies (in Sasine transactions) to all conveyancing deeds.

An important feature of the change is that it is retrospective.[6] So all standard securities are covered, even those executed and recorded before 9 June 2000. This is less surprising than it sounds. In *Beneficial Bank v Wardle*[7] rectification

---

1 Land Registration (Scotland) Rules 1980, SI 1980/1412 r 25.
2 1996 SC 119. An earlier decision, *Bennett v Beneficial Bank plc* 1995 SLT 1105, had been to the same effect.
3 *eg* A J McDonald, *Conveyancing Manual* (6th edn, 1997, by S Brymer, D J Cusine and R Rennie) para 8.11.
4 2000 Act, Sched 12 para 30(23)(a).
5 *Macdonald v Keeper of the Registers* 1914 SC 854. Note that the directions at paras 6.66 and 6.67 of the *Registration of Title Practice Book* (2nd edn, 2000) must be taken to have been superseded by the legislative change.
6 2000 Act, s 77(3).
7 1996 GWD 30–1825.

was allowed under s 8 of the Law Reform (Miscellaneous Provisions) (Scotland) Act 1985 in respect of a standard security in which—as the law was then understood—the security subjects had not been properly described. The rectification sought was to substitute a particular description for a general description. This decision suggested that wherever the description in a standard security fell short of the required standard, the error could be put right by an application for rectification under s 8. In practice this would only be required if the debtor defaulted and the loan was called up. The effect of making the 2000 Act amendment retrospective is not, therefore, to give the heritable creditor a right which he could not obtain by other means. Rather, it is to save the trouble and expense of a s 8 application.

PART V

TABLES

CUMULATIVE TABLE OF APPEALS 2000

This lists all cases digested in *Conveyancing 1999* in respect of which an appeal was heard during 2000, and gives the result of the appeal.

Inverness Seafield Co Ltd v Mackintosh
1999 GWD 31–1497 (OH) (1999 Case (19)) *rev* 2001 SLT 118 (IH) (2000 Case (13))

Kaur v Singh (No 2)
1999 HousLR 76, 2000 SCLR 187, 2000 SLT 1324 (OH) (1999 Case (34)) *affd* 2000 SLT 1323, 2000 SCLR 944 (IH) (2000 Case (26))

Minevco Ltd v Barratt Southern Ltd
1999 GWD 5–266 (OH) (1999 Case (41)) *affd* 2000 SLT 790 (IH) (2000 Case (36))

TABLE OF CASES DIGESTED IN 1999
BUT REPORTED IN 2000

A number of cases which were digested in *Conveyancing 1999* but were at that time unreported have been reported since. A number of other cases have been reported in an additional series of reports. For the convenience of those using the 1999 Volume all the cases in question are listed below, together with a complete list of citations.

Bristol & West Building Society v Aitken Nairn WS
2000 SLT 763, 2000 SCLR 47 (IH)

Cloy v T M Adams & Sons
2000 SLT (Sh Ct) 39; R R M Paisley and D J Cusine (eds), *Unreported Property Law Cases from the Sheriff Courts* (2000) 373

Forsyth v Royal Bank of Scotland
2000 SLT 1295, 2000 SCLR 61 (OH)

Glasgow City Council v Torrance
2000 SLT (Sh Ct) 32

Heritage Fisheries Ltd v *Duke of Roxburghe*
2000 SLT 800 (IH)

Kaur v *Singh (No 2)*
2000 SLT 1324 (OH), 2000 SCLR 187, 1999 HousLR 76
[The appeal in this case is noted in the previous table.]

Keenan v *Aberdeen Slating Co*
2000 SC 81, 2000 SLT 1259 (IH)

McDonald's Tr (Souter) v *Aberdeen District Council*
2000 SC 185, 2000 SLT 985, 2000 HousLR 30 (IH)

Morrison-Low v *Paterson (No 2)*
2000 SLT 624 (IH)

Oliver & Son Ltd Ptnr
2000 SCLR 599 (IH)

Rose v *Bouchet*
2000 SLT (Sh Ct) 170